Falling in Love with Jesus

Abandoning Yourself to the Greatest Romance of Your Life

BY DEE BRESTIN AND KATHY TROCCOLI

W PUBLISHING GROUP™

www.wpublishinggroup.com

A Division of Thomas Nelson, Inc.
www.ThomasNelson.com

Published by W Publishing Group, a Division of Thomas Nelson, Inc., P.O. Box 141000, Nashville, Tennessee 37214.

Unless otherwise indicated, Scripture quotations used in this book are from the Holy Bible, New International Version. Copyright © 1973, 1978, 1984, International Bible Society. Used by permission of Zondervan Bible Publishers.

Other Scripture references are from the following sources:

The Amplified Bible: Old Testament (AMP), copyright © 1962, 1964 by Zondervan Publishing House; and the Amplified New Testament, copyright © 1958 by the Lockman Foundation. Used by permission.

The King James Version of the Bible (KJV).

The New King James Version (NKJV), copyright © 1979, 1980, 1982, 1992, Thomas Nelson, Inc., Publisher.

J. B. Phillips: The New Testament in Modern English, Revised Edition (PHILLIPS). Copyright © J. B. Phillips 1958, 1960, 1972. Used by permission of Macmillan Publishing Co., Inc.

The Message (MSG), copyright © 1993. Used by permission of NavPress Publishing Group.

The Living Bible (TLB), copyright 1971 by Tyndale House Publishers, Wheaton, Ill. Used by permission.

The New Revised Standard Version Bible (NRSV) © 1989 by the Division of Christian Education of the National Council of the Churches of Christ in the United States of America. Used by permission.

Library of Congress Cataloging-in-Publication Data

Brestin, Dee, 1944–
    Falling in love with Jesus : abandoning yourself to the greatest romance of your life / Dee Brestin and Kathy Troccoli.
        p. cm.
    Includes bibliographical references.
    ISBN 0-8499-4236-5
    ISBN 0-8499-4334-5 (tp)
    1. Christian women—Religious life. 2. Love—Religious aspects—Christianity. I. Troccoli, Kathy, 1958–   . II. Title.

BV4527 .B688 2001
248.8'43—dc21   00-064653
                                                                        CIP

Printed in the United States of America
01 02 03 04 05 06 PHX 9 8 7 6 5 4 3 2 1

Dedication

To the Beloved of Christ,
you dear precious women whom we
have the privilege of speaking to, singing to,
writing for, and praying over.

You are the object of His affection.

Contents

Acknowledgments vii

OVERTURE: *When I Fall in Love*

1. A Dream Is a Wish Your Heart Makes 3
2. Someday My Prince Will Come 23
3. Looking for Love in All the Wrong Places 49

ACT I: *First Love*

4. It Had to Be You 75
5. Love Me Tender 101

ACT II: *Wilderness Love*

6. Killing Me Softly 121
7. You Can't Hurry Love 139

ACT III: *Invincible Love*

8. Unforgettable 163
9. Our Love Is Here to Stay 179

Notes 195
Sources for Songs 198
Additional Materials for *Falling in Love with Jesus* 199

Acknowledgments

To the W Publishing team:

We thank each member at W Publishing who has contributed to this endeavor. We especially thank:

Mark Sweeney, David Moberg, and Lee Gessner—for believing in us, listening to us, and catching the excitement for what this could mean in the lives of women.

Ami McConnell and Kathy Decker—for your enthusiasm about the book, and for editing with great sensitivity.

Harry Clayton, Heidi Groff, and Russ Hall—for your commitment to excellence, in being sensitive to capture the unique and passionate content of this book on video.

Debbie Wickwire—you are far more than an author liaison—you are a friend who is indeed respected deeply. How kind of God to have you involved in this project. You possess the very heart of the woman we've portrayed in this book.

To our team:

Matt and Steve—for constantly being men of integrity. It feels so safe to know that you always want to be sensitive to what God desires.

Our faithful prayer teams—for your willingness to place yourself at the feet of Jesus on our behalf.

Linda and Gay—you are priceless.

Dee—

This has been such a beautiful experience for me. You have become a cherished mentor. Thank you for pursuing me, encouraging me, and teaching me. I love you.

Kath

Kathy—

Thank you for saying yes, yes, yes . . . to the book, the video, the friendship. How thankful I am to you for being so vulnerable, so fun, so honest, so passionate . . . How amazing it has been to see the glory of God fall. I love you.

Dee

When I Fall in Love

∿

Orchestra
maestoso e appassionato
(Begin strongly, with majesty, to stir the heart)

1

A Dream Is a Wish
Your Heart Makes

YEARNING. THAT IS THE EMOTION THAT POURS THROUGH THE parchment pages of the journal Kathy Troccoli is writing to the man she prays will one day be her husband:

October 20, 1994

I wonder where you are tonight—I've been praying for you—I wonder if you're yearning for me too . . . Please know I long to hold you, kiss you, share the depths of my soul with you . . . Sweet man of my heart—I go to bed this night with the comfort of knowing you're out there—and the hope that someday we will be together.

I want to dream with you—drink life with you—journey to high places with you.

Please find me.

In making this entry, Kathy is keeping alive a dream that she might one day meet a wonderful man, the man who would be her husband. And on a deeper level, Kathy's journal shows the heart of every woman. No matter our marital status, there is a part in each of us that God created to be a bride. For Scripture is clear that true believers will one day become the Bride of Christ.

When Kathy vulnerably showed me her journal, I thought: *This is perfect. If Kathy will share this we can help women understand the amazing parallel that Scripture makes between falling in love on earth and falling in love with Jesus. If women would yearn for closeness with Jesus the way they yearn for closeness with an earthly mate, their lives would be absolutely transformed.*

When Cinderella sings "A Dream Is a Wish Your Heart Makes," females from nine to ninety sigh. God knows us, He designed us to be uniquely feminine, and He knows how to talk to us. He continually makes a romantic analogy in Scripture, telling us that He is our heavenly Bridegroom.

He woos, He wins, and He weds.

And His heart is broken when we are unfaithful.

Kathy, as a single woman, has taught me so much about approaching the Lord as my Bridegroom. I have typically approached the Lord as my Father, yet Scripture makes both analogies. If we have put our trust in Christ, we are betrothed to Him. Kathy is helping me to understand and cherish this promise from the Lord:

> *As a bridegroom rejoices over his bride,*
> *so will your God rejoice over you.* (Isaiah 62:5b)

Kathy's passionate songs swell with emotion, expressing an intimate relationship with Jesus. A friend commented on her ballad "When I Look at You." She said that it was pretty bold to sing "Hold me, don't let me go, I need you . . ." in that really desperate way about God.

Kathy's response was simply:

But that's the way I live with Him! And that's the way I want to express my relationship with Him to the world—to help them understand that He's as close as our very breath, and we can get that close to Him. Not only that, He desires to be that close to us.[1]

I (Dee) have been married for over thirty-five years. In considering how to draw closer to Jesus, my heavenly Bridegroom, I can draw upon what I have learned from my earthly marriage to Steve. Our marriage has progressed through three stages:

> First love
> Wilderness love
> Invincible love

Most marriages never make it to the third stage. Though couples may stay married, they do not arrive at invincible love. After the exciting time of first love, they get lost in the wilderness. You see these couples in restaurants, consumed with their linguine rather than their love. The tender glances, the laughter, the romance is gone. They may have moments of intimacy together, but basically, those moments are just an occasional rendezvous in the desert.

But there are couples who find their way into the promised land of invincible love. This is absolutely the sweetest place on earth.

Because of God's grace, Steve and I made it through the wilderness and are experiencing a glimpse of invincible love. As in our wonderful first-love stage, we are eager to be together, and we light up when the other walks into the room. But this third stage is deeper, and far better. There is a great joy in knowing and being known, and in the security that our love, no matter what, is here to stay.

The same three stages are true in a believer's relationship to Jesus. Though Kathy and I will refer to many scriptural models throughout this book, our primary model will be Mary of Bethany. As a preview, consider Mary's progression in her love for Jesus:

1. First Love

Mary of Bethany is sitting at the feet of Jesus, hanging on His every word, a picture of a woman in love. Her sister, Martha, wants to drag her into the kitchen, but Mary doesn't want to miss a glance, a word, an inflection of His voice.

2. Wilderness Love

Mary is weeping. Her brother, Lazarus, has died. Though she and her sister sent word to Jesus, He stayed where He was for two days. This is painful. This doesn't make sense. Yet here Mary falls at the feet of Jesus, clinging to Him in the wounds of life.

3. Invincible Love

Mary is convinced that no matter what happens, she will be faithful. Her love wells up and overflows. Here she is abandoning herself by breaking a pint of precious perfume at the feet of Jesus, wiping His feet with her hair, offering Him her worship.

This book will walk you through these three stages. Most believers, sadly, never make it to the third stage. They love the Lord, and they have times of intimacy with Him, but basically their lives are devoid of passion for Him. They are simply having an occasional rendezvous with the One who used to be the Love of their life.

But you can know a tender, mature, and invincible love with Jesus. This should be the goal of your life—for nothing, absolutely nothing under the sun, can compare to the sweetness of mature love with Jesus.

How I remember the first-love stage—both with Steve and then, again, with Jesus.

The First Time Ever I Saw Your Face

The handsome young man in the row behind me at Northwestern University leaned forward, close enough that I caught the scent of

English Leather. Even his whisper was deep and masculine. "Excuse me . . . I've run out of paper. Can you help me out?" Quickly I snapped open my three-ring binder, heart beating, hoping, yet afraid to hope, that this might be a ploy to make contact with me. I smiled as I handed him the paper, and he smiled back warmly. *Hmm, could it be?* After class, when he fell into stride alongside me and introduced himself, I knew. Though I tried to appear nonchalant, as if having a man like this show an interest in me was as usual as having orange juice for breakfast, my thoughts were racing. *Oh my goodness, look at how those extraordinary blue eyes are watching me. He's hanging on my words. He's laughing. Stay cool, Dee. Could this remarkable man, and yes, this is a man, not a boy, could he actually be interested in me?*

We paused under a giant oak near the gothic arches of Deering Library. When I shivered, more from jitters than from the wind from Lake Michigan, he gallantly placed his jacket gently over my shoulders. I looked down at my shoes, willing the flush to stay out of my cheeks. *He's going to ask me out; I feel it coming. Oh my. I can hardly believe someone so amazing is mindful of me, but he is, he is.* During those initial days of our courtship, I awoke each morning with a glow, trying to remember why I felt so full of anticipation: *Something wonderful is happening in my life—what is it? Oh yes, Steve!* I then leaped out of bed enthusiastically and dressed with special care, counting the moments until I would see his face and hear his wonderful masculine voice. Life was sweet, and everybody and everything was colored in the lovely hues of our budding love.

I didn't expect to have the same overwhelming emotions when I gave my life to Jesus Christ a few years later. I knelt in surrender to Him in our Indianapolis bedroom because I was convinced, after a time of searching, that Jesus was God incarnate. It was the fear of the Lord that brought me to my knees in repentance. But then His Spirit simply overwhelmed me. C. S. Lewis said he was "surprised by joy" at his conversion. Likewise, I could hardly believe that the God who made the universe was mindful of me, but it was clear that He was.

"Heaven came down," as the old hymn joyously declares, "and glory filled my soul." He changed my perspective, put joy in my heart, and answered my infant prayers as quickly as a mother lifts her wailing newborn from his crib. Like a smitten schoolgirl, I walked on cloud nine for the next few months, wanting to tell everyone I met about Jesus. I awoke each morning with a glow, trying to remember why I felt so full of anticipation: *Something wonderful is happening in my life—what is it? Oh yes, Jesus!* I leaped out of bed, eager to be with Him, to see what He would whisper to me from His Word. Life was sweet, and everybody and everything was colored with the love we had for each other.

Love Is a Many Splendored Thing

Do you know the secret of overcoming a hundred sins in your life? Of having an inextinguishable joy—no matter the circumstances? It is a secret most believers have missed.

The secret lies not in ten steps, and not in approaching the Bible as a self-improvement guide, but in being deeply in love with Jesus, so that your desire is to be completely abandoned to Him and receive whatever He has for you. Those who learn to relate to Jesus as the Love of their life, on a moment to moment basis, have a vitality surpassing that of most believers and a freedom from sins that once imprisoned them.

Learning to approach Jesus as your Bridegroom may sound foreign to you, but it is a language you, as a woman, were designed to understand.

How to Handle a Woman

In the musical *Camelot,* King Arthur sings "How to Handle a Woman." A wise old man told him the secret, a secret known to every woman. What is it?

It is to love her. Simply love her. Scripture says the same:

Husbands, love your wives, just as Christ loved the church and gave himself up for her. (Ephesians 5:25)

As a member of the relational sex, we long to be loved, we long to be cherished. And we are very interested in romance, in stories where the hero deeply loves and sacrifices for the lady. God knows this, for He made us. And He knows how to talk to us. The whole Bible can be viewed as a wonderful romance.

Both men and women who have put their trust in Christ are called the "Bride of Christ" and need to learn to see themselves as such. And though we are writing primarily to women, we certainly hope men will read this book and be inspired and enlightened by the analogy as well. However, it is easier for women to put themselves into a bride's shoes and to be drawn to the metaphor of romance, for we are typically as enthralled by a good love story as men are by a championship basketball game in overtime. If you saw *Sleepless in Seattle* you may remember the scene when actress Rita Wilson begins recalling, in vivid detail, the lovers' plight in *An Affair to Remember.* As she is transported into the make-believe world of Cary Grant and Deborah Kerr, the men watch her escalating emotion in amazement. Eventually, as her weeping becomes more profuse, their amazement turns to concern, and the question is asked: "Is she all right?"

Later, Meg Ryan and Rosie O'Donnell, watching *An Affair to Remember* over a box of Kleenex, concur: "Men just don't get this movie." But as women, we understand. We love romance. We want every detail. We want to know what he said, what she said. We want the expression on his face described—we want to know everything.

Even in the ancient biblical Book of Ruth, we see it. Ruth returns from her romantic rendezvous with Boaz, which Naomi had orchestrated. Immediately Naomi inquires, "How did it go, my daughter?" And then Ruth "told her *everything* Boaz had done for her" (Ruth 3:16*b*, italics added).

Women are energized by romance, and mysterious truths become clear when spoken in the language of love. And when we realize just how tenderly Jesus loves us, an amazing power in us is unleashed.

We hope this book will be fun for you, like the joyful wedding where Jesus turned water into wine, yet solemn and sacred, like the vows that were exchanged that day. Author Jack Deere has commented that the greatest danger facing the church today comes not from outside the church but from within:

> It is not the New Age or secular humanism that is crippling the church today. It is a lack of love for God, the lukewarmness of the church, that is its greatest enemy. A lukewarm, loveless version of Christianity may succeed in propagating a little religion here and there, but it will never capture the heart of a dying world.[2]

Just as we shouldn't settle for a ho-hum marriage, devoid of passion and joy, we shouldn't settle for a ho-hum relationship with Jesus.

Hopelessly Devoted to You

How do we progress to becoming truly devoted to Jesus, to relating to Him as our Bridegroom? Just as those who want to have a good marriage can learn something by observing others who do, we can learn something from those in Scripture who had a deep love relationship with the Lord. Kathy asked me, "Has this been done? There are so many books, for example, about the women in Scripture, but are there any books that look at individuals in Scripture who had a deep love relationship with Jesus?"

No doubt it has been done, but we want to do it for you with a contemporary slant by making analogies to some captivating earthly romances. Why not use the power of a parable, as Jesus did, to learn heavenly truths from earthly stories? A picture has the power to turn the light on, illuminating mysterious truths and changing our lives.

As women, we are mesmerized by a beautiful love story. Who could not be captivated by the sacrificial love between the husband and wife in the award-winning Italian movie *Life Is Beautiful*? And who of us did not groan when Scarlett O'Hara, in *Gone with the Wind,* ran past knock-your-socks-off Rhett Butler, who truly loved her, for anemic and *married* Ashley Wilkes, who never would? We will learn parallel truths from these and other stories about falling deeply in love with Jesus. Though some may be surprised when we compare Jesus to an earthly "bridegroom," Scripture itself often takes an imperfect man, like Moses, Boaz, or Solomon, and makes him a "type of Christ" for the purpose of illumination. Obviously no one can compare to Jesus, who is altogether lovely, but light can be shed through the power of a parable.

In addition to contemporary love stories, we will look at some of the love stories that God Himself gives us in Scripture, as in Hosea and the Song of Songs. The Song of Songs is an intimate book that Jews were forbidden to read until they were thirty. The Shulammite maiden in the Song of Songs represents you, and it will thrill your soul as you discover just how much Jesus loves you. You are His Bride, His Beloved. The same purity, faithfulness, and abandonment that Solomon, the earthly bridegroom, desired from the Shulammite maiden, Jesus desires from you.

We understand that sometimes the Song of Songs and the subjects of romance can make single women want to flip the switch. Kathy says, "We're tired of books and sermons on marriage, of pastors who drone on and on about what a wife or husband should do and then, like an afterthought, tack on a sentence for singles. They'll close their Bible, and in their deep pastoral voice, say: 'And for those of you who are single, just remember, as you leave today, keep Jesus as your Bridegroom.' At that point I think, *Hey, Buddy, I live there. Every day, that's who Jesus is to me. But aren't we all supposed to live there? Why wasn't that comment included when you addressed the married couples?*"

In this book we will learn *how to live there,* how to relate to Jesus as our Bridegroom. And though we will be looking at earthly romances, please know that our focus is on the ultimate Bridegroom.

This book goes way, way beyond the subject of earthly marriage and romance and is completely relevant to all women, no matter their age or marital status.

Kathy and I have tried to be as vulnerable as we could in this book. We have seen what happens when women open up to other women about their deepest emotions, especially when they have a true yearning for God to come heal, restore, and revive.

I am absolutely delighted to be doing this project with Kathy, and I want you to know why I think she brings so much to this project.

My Life Is in His Hands

Whether it is secular or sacred, when Kathy Troccoli sings a love song, she pours her whole heart into it. When she sings "Embraceable You" in her deep resonant voice, women sigh, as visions of romance with the man of their dreams capture their imaginations. (People are often surprised to discover that a woman as dynamic as Kathy is still single.)

I remember the day Kathy showed me one of her journal entries. I looked into her deep brown eyes for reassurance that she really meant for me to open it. She nodded. "Go ahead, Dee; it's okay. Read it." I opened the cover of the classy leather-bound journal gently, feeling a bit like I was peeking into the window of someone's bedroom.

The first entry was made on an autumn night in 1994.

October 20, 1994 10:15 P.M.

I can't believe I'm finally doing this . . . actually putting my pen to the paper and writing my heart to you . . . you . . . by the time I read this out loud—you'll be here—I'll see your eyes, I'll feel your hair, I'll touch your strong hands, and hear the sound of the voice I'll hear for a lifetime—the voice I've been longing to hear—the voice that will ignite me, soothe me, speak passionately to me . . .

"Oh, Kath," I said, "this is so personal. Are you sure you don't mind?"

"Take it home tonight and read it all," she said. "But if you lose it," she added with her characteristic New York boldness, "I'll kill you."

Carefully I slipped it into the inner pocket of my briefcase and zipped the pocket tightly, realizing Kathy didn't know how often I lose things. (One of my most frequent prayers is "O Lord, please help me find . . .") That night I read the whole journal, weeping as I read, wondering if the Lord had orchestrated all of this. Kathy's yearnings reminded me so much of the opening lines of the Song of Songs, where the Shulammite maiden is expressing her longing for her future bridegroom. *Oh my,* I thought, *this is such a powerful parallel! But will Kathy really be willing to have such personal thoughts published?*

When I came back to Kathy's house the next day, the magazine crew for *Today's Christian Woman* was there, having gone overtime on a photo shoot for their Christmas cover. She heard me open the door and shouted, "Come on up, Dee. We're almost finished. Talk to me—this is the last shoot."

I climbed the steps and sat on the top one, peering into her office as the makeup artist powdered Kathy's nose and the cameraman adjusted his lights. When all was ready, the cameraman said, "Pick up the phone, Kathy. Pretend to talk on it." As if on cue, the phone rang, and she reached for the receiver.

It was a setup. Pamela Muse, with whom Kathy shares a condo in Nashville, was calling on another line from the next room. In a low, old man's raspy voice, she asked, "How's my little kumquat?" Kathy broke into childlike laughter, with her amazing smile, as the photographer clicked away.

And then, right in the midst of the frenzy of cameras, lights, and technicians, Kathy peered over her desk and asked, "Dee, what did you think of my journal?"

I gave her a look, trying to communicate nonverbally that I would prefer to talk about this later! Yet I reassured her, saying, "It's wonderful, Kath. I felt like I was holding your heart in my hands." Pleased, she gave me her crooked little smile.

And yes, Kathy is willing to share her journal with you. Kathy makes herself so vulnerable, a quality that acts as a catalyst, helping us to be honest with ourselves, with each other, and with God. I first became aware of Kathy through the song she'd written, "My Life Is in Your Hands." As her voice soared over my car radio, I thought, *Wow, who is this?* Getting to know Kathy has shown me that she lives what she sings. Her life *is* in His hands, and I have seen her fall back in abandonment to Him, like we used to do as children in that scary game where you'd fall backward into someone's arms, showing how much you trusted him.

Together

"Two are better than one," Solomon tells us, "for they have a good return for their work" (Ecclesiastes 4:9). How true that has been for Kathy and me. God knew what He was doing when He caused our paths to cross, for we are catalysts for each other.

In many surface ways, we are opposites. Kathy is single, and I am married. Kathy is from New York, and I have lived most of my life in the upper Midwest and the last twenty years in a small prairie town in Nebraska. (The first time I heard Kathy in concert in our state, she asked, "Where am I? What do people do in Nebraska?")

We're using song titles for our chapter titles and subheadings (though we are looking at them from God's perspective). In brainstorming for them, we found we not only had different tastes but also had grown up in different eras. I was always reaching back to the classics and suggesting wonderful songs like "I Could Have Danced All Night." Kathy would groan, "Get with it, Dee!" Then she'd suggest some obscure title such as Bonnie Raitt's "I Can't Make You Love Me."

I would protest, "I've never even heard of it."

She'd plead, "Trust me, Dee."

The cool blood of the English and Scots flows quietly through my veins, making me reserved, while Kathy is Italian, and a fiery river of red flows through hers. I found myself often raising an eyebrow at Kathy, cautioning, "I think we might be crossing a line."

"Come on, Dee, loosen up," she'd laugh.

Kathy grew up in a Catholic home and I in a Protestant one. Though both of us, since giving our lives to Jesus as adults, find our primary identity in Christ rather than in a specific denomination, our heritage influences us. Kathy's stories include a special moment with Mother Teresa and an amazing story of a Slovakian priest who was used of God to help her make a difficult choice at a critical moment in her life.

I found I was often reaching to the hymns I'd heard growing up. To my amazement, Kathy had never heard of them. One day I suggested, for a subheading, "He Owns the Cattle on a Thousand Hills."

Kathy looked at me with disbelief. "You're kidding, right, Dee?"

"No, why?"

"He owns the cattle on a thousand hills! Yeah, that's romantic. Surely that can't be a song."

"It is, I promise!"

"They must only sing it in Nebraska. Dee, we're not putting that title in a book about intimacy."

We laughed.

"It really is a song, Kath. Go, get your hymnbook. I'll prove it."

"I don't have a hymnbook."

I was stunned. "Kathy Troccoli doesn't own a hymnbook?"

"I never grew up with all that. We never sang about cattle."

Sometimes we laughed until tears came to our eyes, but we realized the difference in our heritage illustrated the rich diversity in the body of Christ. As we have traveled and ministered throughout the world, we have come to see that there are true believers in every denomination. Though we may have varying styles of worship and differences in peripheral areas, those differences diminish in the light of being made new creations in Christ.

Kathy's sophisticated office is decorated in rich browns, leather, and mahogany, while mine is a floral Laura Ashley. I swallowed hard when she and her friend Pamela told me the story of Kathy being the maid of honor in her dear friend Allyson's wedding.

Half in jest, Kathy had told Allyson there were two conditions: "No pink. No Laura Ashley." Allyson called back a couple of weeks later and said, "Coli, the good news is that your dress is not pink. It's lavender. [As if that helped!] The bad news is that it is Laura Ashley." Being her dramatic self, Kathy let out a long groan and made a face as if someone had forced her to swallow Milk of Magnesia.

Kathy took the brightly colored square-necked Laura Ashley bridesmaid's dress to a seamstress in New York to tighten the bouffant sleeves. ("Because I'm not *bouf*," she said, rolling her eyes. "I already have the shoulders of a football player. I don't need *bouf*.") She also asked to have the "Lucille Ball pleats" going to the drop waist removed. ("Because I'm not pleats either. You have to be as thin as a rail to wear pleats.")

Laughing, Pamela said, "They've never even seen a Laura Ashley dress in Brooklyn." I laughed too, but all the while I was thinking, *Just wait until Kathy sees my office—and the frothy pink Laura Ashley guest room in which she'll be sleeping!* More seriously, I thought, *We're going to need a lot of prayer to help us to be like-minded on this manuscript, or when I'm not looking Kath will take out the* bouf, *the pleats, and who knows what else.*

I am fourteen years older than Kathy and am fast becoming wrinkled and matronly, while Kathy is very striking. (There isn't quite the same pressure on Bible teachers to be breathtaking as there is on Christian singers.) We balance each other. I hope I am helping Kathy remember that all this emphasis in her business on the exterior is vanity, a chasing after the wind, and she is helping me go to pot a tad more slowly.

We both, eventually, will go to pot. But even when we are old and gray, hobbling along on our canes, we will still love romance. There will always be a young girl living in us who hums "When You Wish upon a Star."

Those who are young forget that the elderly are not so very different. My ninety-two-year-old mother-in-law shocked my husband by asking him to take her to the racy, but romantic, movie *Notting Hill*.

(She is so little that the people behind her thought the seat was empty until they heard her laughing, pounding the armrests, and crying, blowing her nose profusely.) We may not be able to see the starry-eyed young girl in the white-haired lady who is shriveled and bent with arthritis, but she is still alive in her soul. No matter our age or marital status, we, as women, love romance.

Some of us, we realize, are prone to be more romantic than others, and Kathy and I have often been categorized as over the top. Kathy says people have said things to her like: "Troccoli, you're such a sap. You're so dramatic."

But she says, "I'm sorry. I admit it. I do like Barry Manilow. I love Karen Carpenter. And yes, even Steve Lawrence and Eydie Gorme."

It is here, in our love for romance, and in our love for our ultimate Bridegroom, where I have found such a sweet connection with Kathy. I love sitting by a crackling fire of fragrant cedar logs on winter nights. Kathy might light candles even when eating her Special K in the morning. When Kathy told her women friends, on vacation, that she wanted to do something romantic, some were baffled, because their definition of romance was limited to a guy and a girl. But though that's part of it, romance is so much bigger than just a love story. Romance has to do with making things lovely because of love. Romance means absorbing the beauty of life: conversation, atmosphere, places, and surroundings. It means increasing our awareness of the fragrance of pine trees, freshly ground coffee, and sheets drying on the line; hearing the music of waves, children's laughter, and the rain drumming on the roof; seeing the signature of God on His creation. It means drinking the gift of life to the dregs. All to be enjoyed, all to be taken in.

I don't want to eat a TV dinner from an aluminum tray; I want to dine on fine china. Don't ask me to be sensible at Christmas. I want lots of tiny white lights, old-fashioned carols, and loving surprises tied in silver packages with glossy red ribbons.

My heart yearns for poetic phrases, perfect snowfalls, and beautiful ballads. My heart was made for romance.

God is romantic. He covers the earth with a canopy of glittering stars and the woods with a profusion of tiny blue forget-me-nots. Sometimes, when I gush about some things, I can almost see people reaching for their imaginary violins. But that's the way I am; that's the way I think; that's the way He made me.

I've made Kathy sing all kinds of songs as we've been working together. And every time, whether it's the opening lines to "When a Man Loves a Woman" (as we worked together on a balcony on Sanibel Island, with the sounds of the waves lapping the shore) or the opening lines to "Someone to Watch over Me" (as we worked over the phone), I sigh, I melt, I am transported to another world.

We know that many women share our romantic hearts, and others will be moved more to do so. But I want you to know that learning to see Jesus as my Bridegroom through the Scripture and through Kathy's eyes has given me so much more joy and victory in my life. Kathy also helps me to be sensitive to those of you who are single, for I am realizing how much you feel like it is a "married world." Women often come up to Kathy after a concert or a women's conference, hold her hand, look her right in her eyes with deep concern, and say, "Kathy, why are you still single?" Kathy's gotten so tired of the question that she often addresses the subject of singleness from the stage:

1. It is not a disease.
2. It doesn't need a cure.
3. Don't give me any more books on "How Not to Be Single."
4. Please don't try to fix me up with your brother-in-law, even though you know he's perfect for me.
5. And don't you dare tell me about what beautiful babies Carmen and I could have together. (Carmen is a single Italian singer.)

Needless to say, having Kathy as a coauthor has made this book very sensitive to singles.

But what initially drew me to Kathy was her ability to feel and see things deeply, especially when they relate to Jesus. She has experienced great sorrow in her life, having lost both parents to cancer, having lost loves, and having struggled with bulimia and depression. She has "leaned into her pain," and it has made her a woman of spiritual depth. Many of you think of Kathy only as a singer, but she is also an author, a songwriter, and a gifted speaker. Neither one of us wants this to be a "fluffy" book, a book of "Christianity lite." We absolutely agree that the power to transform our lives lies in the very words of God, and in giving ourselves in abandonment to the Lord. We are praying that this book will give you a hunger to go deeper, to pull out eternal truths from Scripture, by completing the Bible study workbook and video series.

The Bible study workbook will help you to sit at the feet of Jesus every day. In the corresponding half-hour weekly video, you will be learning from Scripture how to deepen your love relationship with Jesus. I will be teaching and Kathy will be sharing stories and poignant songs. This short video will act as a catalyst for your own small group sharing. We've seen powerful things happen when women get together. They have a unique opportunity to be honest with God and with each other. We pray this won't be just a sentimental journey, but a journey that you can look back on and say, "It was during those ten weeks that I began to really see Jesus in a new way and yearn for an intimacy with Him that I had not known."

Holy, Holy, Holy

When we first described this project to the wonderful men from our team at W Publishing Group, to Dee's husband, and to Kathy's male manager, they were a little uncomfortable with the parallel we were making. We think that is in part because, as a female staff member at Word assessed: "Men often think of intimacy in terms of the sexual relationship, whereas women are more likely to see the bigger relationship picture."

One man suggested we call this book *Falling in Love with God,* because that would be less controversial. Our decision to keep the existing title is based on our reasoning that the Word became flesh, in part, to facilitate a personal relationship with the Deity. When we pray, we think of Jesus, not just because His blood allows us to approach a holy God, but because we can visualize Him. The author of Hebrews tells us that because Jesus became flesh, He can sympathize with our weaknesses. Also, it is Jesus, primarily, who is referred to in Scripture as our Bridegroom, while God is more frequently referred to as our Father.

We want to reassure you, our reader, that we realize that the topic of falling in love with Jesus has sacred boundaries. When we make parallels between earthly romance and heavenly romance, we do so in the fear of God. Yet we also realize how terribly our world has perverted the sacredness of romance. God intended courtship, marriage, and the marriage bed to be beautiful and undefiled, but the world has dumped a load of trash on the pure white sheets. God Himself, in Hosea, in Isaiah, in the Song of Songs, and throughout Scripture, makes the parallel to an earthly love relationship to help us understand not only how He loves us but also how He longs for us to love Him.

We have used discretion in choosing the books and movies that illustrate our points. We realize this is a "gray" area and that some of you will find us either too lenient or too strict, but to the best of our ability, we have used Philippians 4:8 as our standard:

> *Finally, brothers, whatever is true, whatever is noble, whatever is right, whatever is pure, whatever is lovely, whatever is admirable—if anything is excellent or praiseworthy—think about such things.*

Though romances that meet this standard are scarce, they do exist. We hope to introduce you to some exciting books and videos for your own personal pleasure, realizing that, as with anything, they should be read or viewed with discernment and discretion.

A Dream Is a Wish Your Heart Makes

Some of you may feel discomfort with this subject because you do not have or even yearn for a deep love relationship with Jesus. Perhaps your love for Jesus is conceptual, rather than actual. One young woman said, after she heard us speak on this subject, "This is so new to me. I have always known that Jesus loved me, but I never thought about Him longing for me to love Him back!"

There are also many believers who do understand passion for Jesus. Initially, they were enthralled with Him, but sadly the honeymoon is long gone and the mundaneness of life has caused their hearts to grow cold. They are sleeping beneath a blanket of deadness and cannot hear the call of God that says, "Awaken, dear one, and come higher with Me."

When we talk about a mature and lasting passion for Jesus, it can seem as unreachable as a mature and lasting passion seems to some married couples. If this topic makes you feel skeptical or uncomfortable, we plead with you not to walk away, for you will be walking away from the greatest romance of your life.

We will admit to you, as the authors of this book, that we are on this journey with you, for we surely have not arrived! We have each had moments of abandonment, as Mary did when she broke her flask of perfume at Jesus' feet. We have each experienced the incredible euphoria of abandonment, in worship, in submission to the Lord, in confession—yet have we stayed in that state? We cannot tell you that abandonment is where we *live*.

When we first started discussing this topic together, Kathy said to me, "I love Jesus, Dee, but I am not continually abandoned to Him. I'm learning." Likewise, one day I was feeling insecure about writing a book like this when I know I fail the Lord so much.

But God, in His great mercy, reassured me that very morning through the words of the preacher I respect most from the past, Charles Spurgeon:

> It may be that there are saints who are always at their best, and are happy enough never to lose the light of their Father's countenance. I am not sure that there are such persons . . . and I have not traversed that happy land. Every year of my life has had a winter as well as a summer, and every day its night. . . . I confess that though the substance be in us, as

in the teil-tree and the oak, yet we do lose our leaves, and the sap with us does not flow with equal vigour at all seasons.[3]

I thought, *If a giant like Charles Spurgeon could admit to not "living" in the state of continual abandonment, then I can too.*

But we want you to know that we are growing through the models we are examining and through praying, every day, that we would go to higher places with Him. Like the mountain climber who catches a glimpse of the top and is given the inspiration to continue, we have caught a glimpse of invincible love.

Dream big. Pray hard. Jesus is our Prince, and this is no fairy tale.

2

Someday My Prince Will Come

WHEN SNOW WHITE SINGS "SOMEDAY MY PRINCE WILL COME," she isn't dreaming of a guy who will love her and leave her. She wants a genuine Prince Charming, a man of character, someone who will never forsake her and who will whisk her off into the happily ever after.

Likewise, in *Beauty and the Beast*, Belle wants much more than arrogant Gaston, who swaggers about, convinced he is God's gift to women. Though most of the women in town swoon at the sight of handsome Gaston and would happily live in a home decorated by antlers, Belle is different. Belle reads books. And she dreams of a man of depth, sensitivity, and nobility. She dreams of someone who can take her to a wider world.

In *The Music Man,* Marian the librarian brushes her hair each night as she gazes out the window, singing "Goodnight My Someone." Mama thinks it is time Marian lowered her standards, urging her to consider the fast-talking salesman who stopped by that day, because he might be her very last chance! "Oh, Mama!" Marian cries.

Anticipation

Just as God has put within the heart of each of us a yearning to be a bride, there is also a yearning for a bridegroom who is *wonderful*. If we keep that hope alive, we also desire to become the kind of bride who would please such a man.

This kind of anticipation pulses through Kathy's journal entries:

December 2, 1994

I'm doing all I can to prepare myself for you . . .

Lord, make me ready. Let me be a wonderful wife . . . full of grace and femininity—full of all that my husband would need in order to feel loved, comforted, supported, respected, and prayed for . . .

December 22, 1994 9:30 A.M.

Almost Christmas . . . just spent a little time in prayer. Once again, I think of you—I pray that you will grow strong with God yet have His sweet tenderness . . . I pray that you will know me—really know me—and be able to look in my eyes, and read the pulse of my heart. I pray that you will take me far into a "once upon a time."

Come soon, dear one . . . I wait . . .

The phrase "once upon a time" awakens our desire to hear the whole love story, to watch as the girl gets the guy, to sigh at the end as they kiss and walk into the sunset. Does this have anything to do with reality? Or does this happen only in fairy tales?

Many women in the world have allowed this dream, this anticipation, to be snuffed out. Our world is *so* decadent that it mocks the possibility of Prince Charming. Women's hearts have grown cold, their dreams have dried up, and so they settle for profane men with provincial minds and paltry goals. Why don't women wait for someone wonderful? They don't think men like this exist. They think that a man with a foul mouth and a fervor for Bud Light is as good as it gets. And we don't even have to be that extreme. Many women have settled for men who are far less than what God would desire for them because they don't believe that God could, or perhaps would, give them such men. They simply don't believe men like that exist.

Wonderful men *do* exist outside of fairy tales, because of the power of Christ.

When the Holy Spirit is unleashed in a man, there is a strength in him that dwarfs the spiritually anemic. Think of David taking on Goliath, or Peter preaching to the hostile religious leaders, or Dietrich Bonhoeffer standing up against Hitler, or James Dobson tearfully exhorting parents to understand the importance of the Christian family. These men, because of Christ, have a purpose and a passion and a power. Ruth Bell saw that strength in a young man named Billy Graham, whom she met on the campus of Wheaton College when the maples burned red and golden. He talked with compassion about the lost and told her that he yearned to help them know Christ. After a date with Billy, she wrote in her journal:

> I watched his profile as he guided us thru the Chicago traffic (tho he didn't know it). Noted the steel of it, marked the glint in his eyes where the streetlights flashed past. Felt the masterful firmness of his hand beneath my arm as he guided me thru the crowd at the church.[1]

If you didn't have the vision before you married to look for a man of God, you can still pray that God will transform the man you married. I (Dee) wasn't looking for godliness when I married Steve, for neither of us knew the Lord. Yet God in His grace reached out to each of us. I have seen

Steve transformed by God's mighty power. I see the compassion of Christ in Steve, reaching out to me, to our children, and to every person who comes across his path. When a man surrenders to the Spirit of Christ, he is filled with a love and a purpose that turns him into a veritable Prince Charming.

And even if a man like this never comes to sweep you off your feet, even if your husband never surrenders to the power of Christ, there is One who is definitely coming to carry you away, if you have put your trust in Him. Your Prince, your King, is, indeed, coming to get you.

> Let us rejoice and be glad
>> and give him glory!
> For the wedding of the Lamb has come,
>> and his bride has made herself ready. (Revelation 19:7)

Do you know who the Lamb is? It is Jesus. Precious Jesus. And you are His beloved Bride.

Someday My Prince Will Come

John Eldredge and the late Brent Curtis explained, in *The Sacred Romance,* that the Bible, from Genesis to Revelation, is a great romance, a "fairy tale" that is true. Within the context of a classic fairy-tale format, we can see our three stages of love:

1. Once upon a Time (First Love)
2. The Great Betrayal and the Quest for Our Love (Wilderness Love)
3. Happily Ever After (Invincible Love)[2]

Once upon a Time (First Love)

My (Kathy's) "once upon a time" began on August 5, 1978, when I prayed that Jesus would come and live inside my heart. The fact that this God whom I'd seen every Sunday hanging on the cross could be known intimately overwhelmed me. This was all such a revelation to me.

Walking out of church that day, I knew I had an escort. I felt like a beautiful bride, a princess. The perfect man had found me. Men had disappointed me so much, and all of a sudden I was face to face with perfect love and promises that wouldn't be broken. I knew in my spirit that His hand would never let go of mine, and that He had just been waiting for my "Yes." Just as in Dee's story, I woke up each morning trying to remember why I felt so full of anticipation. Something wonderful was happening in my life. What was it? It was Jesus. My "once upon a time" had started; the book had begun; the pages were turning.

The Great Betrayal and the Quest for Our Love (Wilderness Love)

The Great Betrayal. On this earth there is going to be trouble. Storms will come to the forest and the princess will be in danger. A great tree will fall across her path, the wind will whip, and a torrential rain will soak her dress and turn her hair into wet straw. Flying monkeys will come screaming out of the trees, and a snake will slither across her path to try to convince her that God is not good and that she cannot trust her Prince. In romantic movies, from *Camelot* to *Cinderella,* there's got to be trouble in paradise to keep us on the edge of our seats. Will the princess and the prince be reunited?

It is often during trouble, in the wilderness, that we wriggle out of His embrace. We betray Jesus, withdraw from Him, run to things on earth for comfort, and then feel unworthy of His love. We think: *I don't want You touching me because I'm not good enough.*

There are so many times in our life when God will not make sense to us, for trouble comes, and He does not instantly deliver us. How will we respond to the wounds of life, whether they are minor, such as an unkind comment from someone, or major, such as facing breast cancer? Will we wriggle out of His arms because we feel He has let us down? Will we then betray Him, running into the arms of a false lover?

In truth, there isn't one of us who hasn't squirmed our way out of God's arms in the wounds of life and run into adulterous arms, breaking the heart of our Bridegroom. Are you thinking, *What false lovers?* Any time we are continually putting something in our lives over our affection for Jesus, whether it is love for food, hidden sin, a consuming career, or a hundred other things, we are betraying God. God speaks through the prophets, telling us how we have broken His heart. Philip Yancey, in *Disappointment with God,* says, "The words of the prophets sound like the words of a lovers' quarrel drifting through thin apartment walls."[3] God has loved us with such a great love. He cries out through Jeremiah:

> *I remember the devotion of your youth,*
> *how as a bride you loved me*
> *and followed me through the desert.* (Jeremiah 2:2)

Yet we have lost our devotion to Him. We have forgotten our first love. Our ardor has cooled. Jesus cries out in Revelation:

> *You have forsaken your first love.* (Revelation 2:4b)

In our relationship with the Lord, each of us has had times of betrayal. Convinced He did not know what He was doing, we have foolishly run away, into the arms of another, or even of the enemy.

But God doesn't give up on us.

The Quest for Our Love. In balcony scenes from *Romeo and Juliet* to *West Side Story,* the prince pursues the princess. When she cannot believe she is worthy of his love, as in countless versions of *Cinderella,* he comes chasing after her with the glass slipper. Who can forget Kevin Costner (as Robin Hood) or Antonio Banderas (as Zorro) riding in, rescuing the damsel in distress, and carrying her into a happily ever after? In our heart of hearts, isn't this what we long for? That our prince will come through?

Our God is so much more amazing than any Hollywood leading man, or even our idea of Prince Charming. He is perfect, His love never fails,

He is omnipotent, and best of all, He is not just some historical figure from the past—He is alive today. Peter put it like this:

> For we have not been telling you fairy tales when we explained to you the power of our Lord Jesus Christ and his coming again. My own eyes have seen his splendor and his glory. (2 Peter 1:16 TLB)

When you think of trouble coming to paradise in romantic movies, you're always thinking about the girl and the guy, and if and when they're going to get together. Jesus, one way or another, always, always gets to us.

Sometimes our Lord comes with a miracle, as He did for Mary of Bethany when He raised her brother, Lazarus, from the dead. Sometimes He simply gives us the grace to face the difficulties of life. I (Kathy) remember when my mother was hospitalized with cancer. Jesus got to me. It wasn't with a miracle, but He made His presence known. I tell the story in my book *My Life Is in Your Hands*.

"Kathy," the doctor began, soberly, "there wasn't just *one* tumor. There are multiple cancerous tumors throughout your mother's liver." I held on, still wanting a word of hope. But then he crushed that hope, saying, "I'm sorry. There's not much we can do."

"What does this mean?"

"Six months to two years," he answered.

I felt faint as so many emotions found their way through every part of my body. I thought about my dad, who died of colon cancer at forty-six years old. I thought about my mom's suffering. I thought about being orphaned.

I walked through the lobby toward a small chapel. No one was in the room, and I fell across one of the pews—facedown, on my stomach. The sound of my weeping filled the room. In my mind, I found myself looking out over a mountaintop. One side was full of a valley of voices rising in chorus: "What's the use? Haven't you had it? Aren't you sick of all this cancer?" On the other side of the mountain was the reminder of all I'd known Jesus to be since 1978.

Then, to my surprise, His voice seemed to break through it all like lightning through a pitch-black sky:

"Am I not still God?"

"Am I not *still* God?"

I lay there motionless, and my breathing was quieted. I knew I could not leave that chapel and meet my mother after her surgery without responding to God's question. Deep inside, I knew that my answer would not only affect me but would affect the last year of my mother's life. With swollen eyes and drenched face, I looked up to heaven and said, "Yes, Lord, You are still God."

Had I turned my back on God and left that question hanging in the air that day, I know that all I would have given my mother during the last year of her life would have been anger, bitterness, and fear.

My taking His hand in trust allowed me to walk alongside my mother and give her a supernatural comfort, peace, and hope. The exchange between us during that time will be forever etched on my heart. The whole dying process, ironically enough, was filled with Jesus' life. He met us at every turn—not without agonizing tears, questions, and long painful days, but He was there. During the final hours of my mother's life, I read Psalm 23 to her as she took deep breaths to recite it with me. She then led a room full of family and friends in the Lord's Prayer.[4]

My Prince came through. And He will for you too. Always. Sometimes with a momentous miracle, sometimes in the mundane minutes of life. He brought Lazarus back to this earth. He brought my mother into eternal life. He came through. He surrounded me with a holy peace during my deepest sorrow—and He will for you as well.

Happily Ever After (Invincible Love)

Once we have trusted Jesus with the wounds of our life, we have begun our move toward mature love. This is not perfect love, but a strong and steady love. Nor does this mean that life will now be easy. Instead, we will continue to have trouble. Jesus promised not that life would be easy but that He would be with us. He said:

In this world you will have trouble. But take heart! I have overcome the world. (John 16:33*b*)

How has He overcome the world if we still struggle with disease, failed relationships, and our own sin nature? I (Kathy) made the choice to give my life to Jesus in 1978. And I'll often say:

> Has life been rosy?
> Has it been smooth sailing ahead?

But those aren't the right questions. The right questions are

> Has God been sovereign?
> Has He been a Keeper of His Word?
> Has He been trustworthy?
> Has He been faithful?

"Yes! Yes!" Always, a resounding "Yes."
We often ask:

> Why are my circumstances so difficult?

We should ask:

> Is God in my circumstances?
> Is He capable of giving me peace, hope, and perspective?

Again, of course, "Yes." He is our Prince who comes through. Paul put it like this:

We are handicapped on all sides, but we are never frustrated; we are puzzled, but never in despair. We are persecuted, but we never have to stand it alone; we may be knocked down but we are never knocked out! Every day we experience something of the death of Jesus, so that we may also know the power of the life of Jesus in these bodies of ours. . . .

We know sorrow, yet our joy is inextinguishable. (2 Corinthians 4:8–11; 6:10a PHILLIPS)

Paul reached the stage of invincible love. How did he get there? He was absolutely convinced that the One to whom he had committed himself was able to do what He had promised.

To Dream the Impossible Dream

It is easy to say, intellectually, that Jesus is good, that He cares for us, and that He will do what is best in our lives. It is another thing for these truths to get to the heart, so that we are free from fear and anxiety no matter the circumstances.

How can we possibly get to this point? One of the things God tells us to do is to look back in the past and see how He was faithful in the lives of other believers, and in our own lives. Therefore, we'd like to share with you the true stories of two women, women who saw their Prince come through, women who arrived at invincible love, that state where you can trust, no matter the circumstances.

Come Rain or Come Shine

As told in the first chapter of the Book of Luke, Elizabeth, the wife of Zechariah, longed to be a mother. But it didn't happen. All of her life she waited, watching her friends with precious babies and wondering if her arms would ever hold her own. I (Kathy) have often felt the lonely sting of watching friends fall in love. The euphoria on their faces, the joy in their smiles, and the excitement that seeps into every conversation makes me feel like I am once again watching a romantic movie and eating popcorn all by myself. Don't misunderstand me. I know how blessed I am to have friends that are truly family to me. I have very rich relationships. But I'd be a liar to say there aren't days, especially when the holidays roll around, when I am in the midst of a festive celebration and suddenly feel like Little Orphan Annie out in the cold looking in the window at someone else's warm and wonderful life.

Elizabeth had to listen to her friends talk about their kids for most of her life, but her arms remained empty. Because her culture so tied a woman's worth to childbearing, she felt shame. Yet, even then, the evidence is strong that she trusted God's sovereignty. She didn't shut Him out. One of the characteristics of someone who "practices the presence of God" is that he or she draws near, in dialogue with Him, no matter the circumstances. Perhaps Elizabeth wandered along the hills outside of Jerusalem crying out to God:

Do You still love me, Lord?
Are You still good?
Are You still God?
And if You never give me the deepest desire of my heart, will I still trust You?
Will You ever, ever come through for me?

Two key *b* words that God uses for Elizabeth are significant. He says she is *blameless* in His eyes, and then, a heartbeat later, He says she is *barren*. Note how she is introduced in the Gospel of Luke:

Both [Elizabeth and Zechariah] were upright in the sight of God, observing
all the Lord's commandments and regulations blamelessly. (Luke 1:6)

Wow! They were *blameless* in the sight of God. This doesn't mean they never failed, never sinned, but it does mean they walked in the light and kept short accounts with God. Eugene Peterson puts it like this:

Together they lived honorably before God, careful in keeping to the ways of the
commandments and enjoying a clear conscience before God. (Luke 1:6 MSG)

We often assume, though this is absolutely wrong theologically, that if someone is living wholeheartedly for God her life will be free of trouble. That's why the next *b* word describing Elizabeth may seem surprising:

> But they had no children, because Elizabeth was barren; and they were both well along in years. (Luke 1:7)

Trouble in paradise. There are no babies bouncing on their knees, no music of children's laughter ringing in their home. Menopause comes, the biological clock stops, and their arms are still achingly empty. Perhaps the enemy slithered in, whispering, "You see, your Prince is not coming. He cannot be trusted." Yet, one day, when the dream seemed most impossible, Gabriel, the archangel of good tidings, appears to Zechariah, announcing:

> Do not be afraid, Zechariah; your prayer has been heard. Your wife Elizabeth will bear you a son, and you are to give him the name John. He will be a joy and delight to you, and many will rejoice because of his birth, for he will be great in the sight of the Lord. (Luke 1:13–15)

Zechariah, however, argues with Gabriel:

> Do you expect me to believe this? I'm an old man and my wife is an old woman. (Luke 1:18 MSG)

Imagine Gabriel's surprise! When Zechariah demands confirmation, Gabriel, in essence, thunders: "Zechariah, I am Gabriel! Have you forgotten that I stand in the presence of an Almighty God? Do you really *dare* to ask for a confirmation?" Then Gabriel pauses. When he speaks, he says, sternly:

> And now you will be silent and not able to speak until the day this happens, because you did not believe my words, which will come true at their proper time. (Luke 1:20)

Zechariah turns white, loses his voice, and, as we see later, loses his hearing as well. He has nine months to think about doubting the archangel.

But Elizabeth believes. She had never completely given up on the impossible dream, and her response is one of great joy and relief. Her Prince has come through!

> *She went off by herself for five months, relishing her pregnancy. "So, this is how God acts to remedy my unfortunate condition!" she said.* (Luke 1:24 MSG)

God doesn't always give us the husbands or the babies for which we pray. But He will give us access to all we need to live an abundant life. We have met thousands of women who share with us the sorrow of not being able to conceive. Our first response is always to pray, because God can do miracles. But we've learned that when God says "No," He will always provide a greater "Yes." So although you may be a "barren woman," with Jesus you can be pregnant with love, and in that, you will be able to deliver His life to all those around you.

I (Kathy) am realizing at forty-two that I may never have a child. But God has repeatedly brought me stories from women who have chosen life over an abortion as a result of hearing my song "A Baby's Prayer." At a concert in Dallas, the organizers planned a beautiful surprise for me. I had just finished singing a song when a twenty-one-year-old woman began to speak over the loudspeaker. She talked about a time when she was pregnant with her second child and was being encouraged to abort the baby. During that time, she had come to see me in concert. I'd sung "A Baby's Prayer":

> But if I should die before I wake
> I pray her soul you'll keep
> Forgive her, Lord
> She doesn't know
> That you gave life to me

The Holy Spirit used the truth in that song to clinch her decision. She kept her baby.

After she shared her story, the young woman walked out on stage to greet me. The audience grew very quiet. In the woman's arms was a newborn baby. His name was Charlie. I began to weep so hard that my mascara started running. I looked like Alice Cooper. Never before had I had to leave the stage to regain my composure. That night was a first.

So although I may never have a child, God has shown me that more children have been born through that song than could ever come through my womb. And in that I rejoice.

When we trust God, when we walk in His light, He empowers us to be a life-giving force to others. And there is absolutely more than one way to give life. Elizabeth was certainly a life-giving force to Mary, the teenager who was called to be the mother of Jesus.

Mary, Did You Know?

How much did Mary actually understand? To be chosen to be the mother of the Messiah was every Jewish maiden's dream. Mary's response of faith is significant:

> *"I belong to the Lord, body and soul,"* replied Mary, *"let it happen as you say."* (Luke 1:38a PHILLIPS)

But did Mary have any idea how hard her life would be? How could she have glimpsed the dark waters ahead? I (Dee) remember how apprehensive I was giving birth to my firstborn—yet I was surrounded by skilled nurses, doctors, and even a husband who was a medical student. Mary was going to give birth to *her* firstborn without even a midwife's help. And did Mary have any premonition her son would be so hated? When He was just a toddler, she had to flee in the night to Egypt. Can you even imagine? And did she know that one day, she would watch His agony on the cross?

We doubt she ever imagined any of this. But God knew it all and cared so deeply. He prepared her for the dark waters ahead. He gave Mary a strong hint to go see Elizabeth. Three months with a woman like Elizabeth, a woman who had passed through the dark waters triumphantly, was exactly what His princess needed.

None of us knows what the future holds. But God wants us to put our hand in His and walk around the corner. That's what we see in Mary's life. When Gabriel told her that "even Elizabeth, her relative, is with child," Mary's first response was to *hurry* to go see Elizabeth. How sensitive she was to following God!

This wasn't a walk down the block, it was a seventy-mile journey. Did Mary struggle with doubts as she traveled? Did she wonder: *Is this really happening? Did Gabriel really appear and tell me I have been chosen to be the mother of the Messiah? Or was I hallucinating?* If she had any doubts, she must have also reasoned: *But if Elizabeth is pregnant—and she'd be showing at six months—then I'll know. Gabriel appeared—and all he said will come to pass. Oh, I must see Elizabeth.*

Mary finally arrives at Elizabeth's home. She knocks gently on the door. When Elizabeth opens it, is she surprised to see Mary? In *The Book of God: The Bible as a Novel,* Walter Wangerin imagines the scene:

Her dark brows were lifted in an intense appeal, and her eyes were filled with beseeching. Clearly, she had come with a question.

Then several things happened so swiftly that they were all one thing, and that thing was the revelation of God.

Mary's eyes dropped to Elizabeth's breasts and then to her belly. In the softest of whispers, she said, "Hail, Elizabeth."[5]

Then, before Mary can even get the words out of her mouth to tell Elizabeth her news, Elizabeth stuns her, because the Holy Spirit has filled her mouth with a prophecy:

> *Blessed are you among women, and blessed is your child! What an honor it*
> *is to have the mother of my Lord come to see me!* (Luke 1:42–43 PHILLIPS)

Did Mary think: *Elizabeth knows! I'm not showing, but she knows. This is really happening. This is really true! Can it be that we are at the start of something so amazing?*

Ecstatically, Elizabeth continues, saying that her baby has leaped has "jumped for joy"! And then she affirms Mary for trusting God, saying:

> *Oh, how happy is the woman who believes in God,*
> *for he does make his promises to her come true.* (Luke 1:45 PHILLIPS)

Their Prince has come through in miraculous ways. Now it is Mary's turn to sing, and sing she does:

> *I'm bursting with God-news;*
> *I'm dancing the song of my Savior God.*
> *God took one good look at me, and look what happened—*
> *I'm the most fortunate woman on earth!*
> *What God has done for me will never be forgotten,*
> *the God whose very name is holy, set apart from all others.*
> *His mercy flows in wave after wave*
> *on those who are in awe before him.*
> (Luke 1:46–50 MSG)

Mary is dancing to the song of her Savior God, and so can we. The euphoria these women feel is the euphoria of women who have fallen deeply in love with the Lord, and they know, because they have passed through the stormy waters triumphantly, that their love is going to last. *His* love is going to last. They have reached the land of invincible love—not a land that is free of trouble, but a land full of confidence and joy.

What each of us desires, what each of us has been created for, is a love that will never end. We want the kind of love Kathy sings about in her Christmas ballad "Only, Always":

> The tree is lit, the fire burns
> The snow is falling but you're keeping my heart warm
> The music plays, the candles glow
> And as you look at me I've got to let you know
>
> It's Christmas time, my darling
> And all I can say
> Is I'll love you
> For only always . . .

Yet as sweet as love songs can be, there is a song that is sweeter. Do you know what that is? It is the book in the Bible called the Song of Songs. Solomon composed a thousand and five songs (1 Kings 4:32), but this song is the best. The phrase "Song of Songs" is like "King of Kings," or "Holy of Holies." It means "the very best."

Some believe the Song of Songs is *only* a literal picture of the beauty of married love and the ecstasy of the marriage bed. When Dee's assistant, who is a single woman, heard that, she exclaimed, "I certainly hope that isn't true—because that means I have missed the best. And you know what? I know I haven't! No man can possibly compare to Jesus."

What is the very best love in life? It is a deep love relationship with Jesus. Many godly men and biblical scholars, including Saint Augustine, Charles Spurgeon, Matthew Henry, and Hudson Taylor, see the allegory in the Song of Songs. Dr. John Phillips compares it to the parables of Jesus, an earthly story with a heavenly meaning, explaining:

Undoubtedly it has a strong historical base, but it is more than a senti-mental ballad. A mere song, no matter how moving and beautiful, could not stand shoulder to shoulder with Isaiah, for instance, unless it had some spiritual truth to impart.[6]

What is the spiritual message, the analogy of the Song of Songs? Beneath the figure of Solomon, the bridegroom king, glimmers Jesus. Just as Solomon loved the Shulammite maiden and was on a quest to bring her into a higher and deeper love, so Jesus longs to take us to a higher and deeper place. When you realize that you are the Shulammite maiden and that your Prince is pursuing you, you will feel so chosen and cher-ished by God. He longs for you to come into invincible love, into the "happily ever after." (We are talking about much, much more than sal-vation!) At the end of the Song of Songs the Shulammite maiden is at the point of total abandonment, so that she can say, with confidence:

> *Many waters cannot quench love;*
> *rivers cannot wash it away.* (Song of Songs 8:7)

To whet your taste for the Song of Songs, we'd like you to take a look at the Shulammite maiden in her first-love stage, her "once upon a time" stage, and see if you can see yourself in her. In this first stage, she is just getting to know the man who is pursuing her and she can hardly believe it is all happening.

Will You Still Love Me Tomorrow?

King Solomon has discovered the Shulammite maiden as he has been rid-ing around his kingdom, surveying all that he owns. Her mother has a vineyard in Solomon's kingdom, and she is working in it. The king comes riding in on his white horse and spies this lovely young maiden. Her hands are stained with grape juice and her skin is darkened by the relent-less sun, yet all he sees is her beauty, and he is smitten. She can hardly believe the king is taking notice of her. She is immediately self-conscious about her appearance:

> Do not stare at me because I am dark,
>   because I am darkened by the sun.
> My mother's sons were angry with me
>   and made me take care of the vineyards;
>   my own vineyard I have neglected. (Song of Songs 1:6)

Just as the Shulammite maiden felt unworthy when she was aware of the attentions of the king, so do we feel unworthy and fearful when we are first aware of the attentions of our holy King. As we glimpse His purity, His bright light illumines all the blemishes and dark places in our character.

We have seen dynamic things happen at women's conferences. When women look around the room and realize they're all carrying baggage, they feel safe enough to open up. And during the course of the day words of life are spoken and they begin to realize the truth about how God sees them. They are His Beloved. Period. That enables them to be honest about where they've been, what they've done, and who they are. That's when the deepest wounds or secrets are able to come to the surface: the abortion twenty-five years ago, the bitterness that's held against an ex-husband, the sister they haven't talked to in years.

We watched in wonder as that happened so profoundly at our first seminar on *Falling in Love with Jesus*. After Kathy sang "A Baby's Prayer," the altar was flooded with weeping postabortive women. After Dee shared the story of Mary of Bethany and her total abandonment to the Lord, half of the women in attendance came forward, with an earnest desire to abandon whatever it was that was keeping them from invincible love with Jesus.

We have an infected wound that we don't want lanced. And so we keep changing the bandages instead of running to God and saying, "Heal me, Lord—whatever it takes." We hide and we keep on hiding. Like Adam and Eve, God speaks to us: "Why are you doing that? I see it all." He wants us to come forward with abandonment.

The Shulammite maiden cried, "Do not stare at me!"
Likewise, when Isaiah saw the Lord in His holiness, he cried:

Woe to me! . . . I am ruined! For I am a man of unclean lips, and I live among
a people of unclean lips, and my eyes have seen the King, the LORD Almighty.
(Isaiah 6:5)

As soon as Isaiah confessed his uncleanness, a seraph flew to him
with a live coal, which he had taken with tongs from the altar of sacrifice. He touched Isaiah's mouth and said:

See, this has touched your lips; your guilt is taken away and your sin atoned
for. (Isaiah 6:7)

That is exactly how I (Dee) felt the November day I knelt and surrendered my life to Christ. I didn't *expect* any bells, but, oh! It was as if
it was Christmas Day and the bell towers from all over the countryside
wouldn't stop ringing. The moment I told God that I understood Jesus
had died on the cross to pay for my sins, and that I was ready to receive
His gracious payment, I felt like a heavenly light had fallen upon me.

As wonderful as it was, that same light also illumined the dark cor-
ners in my heart that I hadn't even known existed. I didn't like what I
saw. Like Isaiah, I thought, *Woe is me!* I felt dirty, dark, and unworthy. But
I knew God touched me with the power of Christ's sacrifice; I knew I was
a new creation, clean and forgiven. I did feel like a holy Bride. I believed
it because He told me so. God assured me of His power to cleanse, just
as He assured Isaiah:

> *"Come now, let us reason together,"*
>   *says the LORD.*
> *"Though your sins are like scarlet,*
>   *they shall be as white as snow."* (Isaiah 1:18)

Do I stay convinced that I am His Beloved? No, I vacillate. I fail Him and wonder how He can still love me. Some days I ignore His voice and wonder if He'll ever speak to me again. When I yell at my teenager, or when I receive an angry letter from a reader, or when I pass a store window and see the reflection of a middle-aged woman (*Could that really be me?*), I struggle with my loveability. (Kathy says that when those feelings come, we are allowed to reason with the Lord. Don't ever be afraid to ask Him to reassure you of His love and to reveal Himself in ways you haven't known.)

When I (Kathy), an Italian girl from New York, moved to Nashville in the early 1980s, I felt like Rizzo in *Grease*. There were so many blondes, and the makeup was different: lighter and a lot of pinks. Women wore baby-blue shirts and argyle socks. It just was a different culture. I'll never forget going to a Color Me Beautiful party, where they decide which colors look good against your skin and hair color. I felt so out of place. Everyone there was so feminine and sweet. They were really well meaning, but I remember feeling such shame. I was mortified as they laid different pastels on me and asked, "Are you a spring or an autumn?" (It doesn't take a rocket scientist to figure out that I'm a winter.) Not only was my Mediterranean look out of place, I had a bad perm, wore too much mascara, and was a tomboy. I wanted to crawl under the sofa.

As women, we all deal with "body stuff," with some kind of inadequacy about our appearance. And I think we bring that shame into our relationship with the Lord. We all have things that make us feel insecure. I have struggled with my singleness—I never thought I would be single at the age of forty-two. I have struggled with losses. I didn't expect my mother and my father to get cancer. So I call out to God and ask Him to help me with these heartaches, and to reassure me of His love. He continues to comfort me. He continues to teach me to trust Him.

Jesus sees us through adoring eyes. He sees us cleansed in Him. And He sees our potential. We are the Shulammite maiden, and we are as lovely in His eyes as Cinderella was to the prince. She, too, had trouble believing her loveliness. She fled at midnight, thinking her loveliness lay in her dress. But her prince pursued her, just as our Prince pursues us. He is on a quest for our love. And yes, He will still love us tomorrow.

This is the Song of Songs, the sweetest song.

That's What Friends Are For

Though this book can be read on your own, we are so praying it will whet your taste to get the workbook and video and do them together with your sisters in Christ. Just as one log alone has trouble burning brightly, so will you, alone, have trouble keeping the flame alive. The fellowship of sisters in Christ, particularly sisters who are longing to grow, is like bellows on a smoldering flame.

Many of us have sought out mature Christian women who will sharpen us and hold us accountable. We pray that you too will seek out such women and ask them to do this romantic adventure with you. Being held accountable by our sisters in Christ can sometimes be hard, but spiritual growth will come when we are confronted with the truth.

One of the most intriguing aspects of the Song of Songs is how the Shulammite maiden and the "daughters of Jerusalem" sharpened each other. In the Song of Songs, the daughters of Jerusalem are learning to love the bridegroom as well. They love him through the testimony of the Shulammite, and they, in return, often act as a catalyst for her love, making her flame leap higher and higher as they sing:

> *We rejoice and delight in you;*
> > *we will praise your love more than wine.* (Song of Songs 1:4*b*)

We'd like to make a contemporary parallel to the "daughters of Jerusalem." At many colleges, the women students have a ceremony to announce an engagement. Dee's daughter Sally described the tradition at Taylor University, a Christian school in Indiana.

"Occasionally we'd see a sign in the lobby of our women's dorm announcing:

Ring-Down Tonight!

All three hundred and fifty of us would come. No one wanted to miss it. We didn't know who had just become engaged—we only knew which wing she lived in, for that wing made a circle in the center of the room. Then a candle with the engagement ring was passed slowly around the circle. When it finally came to the engaged girl, she would blow it out. There'd be shrieking, exclamations, hugs, and tears."

One night Sarah King, one of Sally's dearest friends, blew the candle out. Like the Shulammite maiden, this dark-haired beauty excitedly told her story:

> You know how much I have wanted Jeff to propose, for he is the man of my dreams: godly, caring, good-looking, and oh, so wonderful! Well, this weekend, it happened!

The girls of English Hall, like the daughters of Jerusalem, pleaded, "Tell us!"

> We took a picnic to Brown County when he opened up his Bible and started reading to me from 1 Corinthians 13. I tried to keep my hopes from soaring by talking to myself, saying, "Sarah, take it easy—this might not be it."

> But when he took my hand and asked me to come over and sit on the picnic table, his hand was clammy. So that was when I knew.

There was delighted laughter. Sarah continued, with drama:

> He took my sandals off, pulled a cloth out, dipped it in a bowl of water, and began to tenderly wash one foot, then the other. He told me he wanted to serve me and love me as Christ had served and loved the church.

There were sighs. Sarah began to weep as she concluded:

And then he asked me to be his wife!

The Song of Songs could be viewed as an elaborate "Ring-Down." The daughters of Jerusalem draw out the Shulammite maiden with questions, praise her love more than wine, and act as a wonderful catalyst for her love. In the following scene, imagine the Shulammite maiden standing in the middle of the circle, her candle extinguished and her eyes aglow.

> *My lover is like a gazelle or a young stag.*
> > *Look! There he stands behind our wall,*
> *gazing through the windows,*
> > *peering through the lattice.*
> *My lover spoke and said to me,*
> > *"Arise, my darling,*
> > *my beautiful one, and come with me.*
> *See! The winter is past;*
> > *the rains are over and gone.*
> *Flowers appear on the earth."* (Song of Songs 2:9–12a)

If we remember that the Song of Songs is also a picture of our relationship with Jesus, we can see in the above verses His wooing us into a more intimate relationship with Him. He promises that if we arise and go with Him, if we are willing to leave our comfort zone, then the winter of our soul will be past and the joy and power of the resurrection, as shown by the signs of spring, will be ours. It is the Song of Songs—the greatest love story.

Did you know that the Song of Songs has its opposite in the Bible? Instead of the "song of songs," the theme is the "vanity of vanities," and it is the saddest song. It was also written by Solomon, but by that time he was an old man filled with regret. He had suffered the consequences of ignoring God's warning not to marry foreign wives. Solomon had had it all, including the wonderful peace of God, but he gave it up and went looking for love in all the wrong places. He wasted his wisdom, his wealth, and his life. He gave up the peace that passes understanding.

I (Kathy) have learned that nothing, absolutely nothing, is worth sacrificing the peace of God. I will tell you about lines I've crossed and what I've learned. And I (Dee) won't leave Kathy alone out there, just watching her bleed. I will make myself vulnerable as well.

3

Looking for Love in All the Wrong Places

WHAT EACH OF US LONGS FOR, SOLOMON TELLS US, IS UNFAILING love (Proverbs 19:22*a*). We yearn to be cherished for who we are. We dream of a love that will stay fresh, new every morning, and because of grace, will never, ever die. This is the longing of every heart, a longing Kathy expresses in her journal:

> *October 25, 1994 12:24* A.M.
>
> *Just saw Love Affair tonight with Ellie . . . the remake of An Affair to Remember. Warren Beatty and Annette Bening . . . what a beautiful movie—and of course I cried . . . The scenes, the music, their chemistry, undying love . . . but most of all the thought of you . . .*
>
> *Would you, could you . . . will you . . . love me like that?*

Yet Solomon also tells us that unfailing love is exceedingly rare:

Many a man claims to have unfailing love,
but a faithful man who can find? (Proverbs 20:6)

Where Is Love?

When you are dating, sometimes you wonder if you will ever find true love. Can you remember a miserable date, when you weren't clicking with the guy, when he was actually bugging you, and when the evening loomed ahead like an endless lecture from a monotone professor who had not even a fleeting thought that it might be nice if he asked you a question? Or the opposite: You felt like Barbara Walters trying to draw him out. "Yes," "No," and "Maybe" were his best answers. Kathy speaks in her journal of the misery of dating:

October 26, 1997

I have been so disappointed in dating. I don't like feeling stronger than most of the men I've dated. I don't like starting from "How many brothers and sisters do you have . . ." I wish they could know my soul the way my close women friends do. Sometimes the thought of dating makes me feel so tired.

Will I ever meet him? Will this pain go away?

Sometimes I think my capacity to feel deeply gives my life a bit more torture . . . the suffering can go to incredible depths . . . Yet I don't want to despise the things that cause me to become holy—so I drink life to the dregs, love people, love laughing—love affecting the eternal in human hearts . . . but I so feel the ache.

I have to go on a date today. I am so not into it. But I have committed to it.

Will I ever read this to you? Or are my writings in vain?

In the same way, before the Lord finds us, we may try different things to fill up the emptiness in our lives. We may even have "dates" with other religions, but we find ourselves "coming home" disappointed. If we try to fill up the emptiness in our lives with things in the world, we may be satisfied momentarily, but then, like the author of Ecclesiastes, we cry, "All of it is meaningless, a chasing after the wind" (2:17b). We so feel the ache. The end of the pursuit is devastating, for we find ourselves even emptier than when we began.

So Far Away

Kathy has experienced the devastation of failed love. The painful story she told me reminded me of the movie *The Way We Were*, in which Barbra Streisand plays Katie, a radical war protester, and Robert Redford plays Hubbell, an Ivy League yuppie. The kind of girl Hubbell really wants is an upper-class beauty with silky hair, classic features, and an ability to be gracious and charming. Instead, he is mesmerized by Katie, who is none of the above. Katie is consumed with her fight for justice, with ending the war in Vietnam, and with changing the world. Hubbell is drawn by Katie's passion, her charisma. To her astonishment, this amazingly handsome and winsome man pursues her. Yet Hubbell's love, like a beautiful soaring kite, suddenly dies and dives, crashing to earth. As Hubbell withdraws, Katie pursues, trying to make him love her by ironing her hair, restraining her political passion, and yelling, "Nobody will love you, Hubbell, the way I do!"

"I know that, Katie," he says, sadly. But in the end he walks away, marrying a classic American beauty. All that remains for Katie and Hubbell are "Memories . . ." of the way they were. As the collage of images from their love affair float by on the screen, they are deceptively beautiful. The physical beauty of Hubbell drew Katie, but it was a tender trap. Katie was chasing a man who didn't really appreciate her for who she was, who couldn't give her unfailing love, and who, in the end, walked away and broke her heart. We are vulnerable as women. Charm and beauty can fool us, cloaking a lack of character or a lack of real love. It can all be so deceptive when you are in the midst of it.

Kathy longs to be loved for who she is. Her celebrity, charisma, and hectic schedule create a challenge for most men. Her friend Ellie told me, "Guys are either completely intimidated by her, or they come riding in planning to tame this wild filly. Who wants either of those kind of guys?"

Wrapping her arms around her slender legs, Kathy put her head down, hesitating. Then she told me, "Part of me doesn't want to tell this story, because it's *still* painful and because I don't want this man to know how devastated I was. But another part of me, the deepest part of me, is learning to die to myself. I know there's a vital parallel here, about how the wrong paths can seem so alluring and how important it is to obey the Spirit's first prompting. I didn't at this particular time in my life. It was as if I buckled myself into a roller coaster expecting to feel exhilarated, and all the while the car was not quite on the track. It led to destruction. I deceived myself, saying the cost couldn't be that high when, in reality, the cost was *heartbreakingly enormous*."

So, here it is, from Kathy's heart.

I Can't Make You Love Me

Ellie and I were just becoming friends. She was telling me about a guy she had dated in college for a while.

I said, "Ellie, don't pawn off any of your 'ex's' on me."

We laughed.

Ellie said, "But he's Italian."

I smiled. "Probably a *My Cousin Vinny* type."

"No, not at all! He's a very classy guy. All the things we love in an Italian man and none of the things we detest."

"Where is he spiritually?"

"He was close to the Lord once, and he led a campus Bible study, but he's fallen away."

That should have been it. But I left the door open a crack.

Ellie and her husband, Frank, had maintained a friendship with him, and he'd call and even visit sometimes. Once when I was at Ellie's, he phoned, and she said his name pointedly and gave me a look that communicated, *Do you want to talk to him?*

I nodded, smiling. *This could be fun,* I thought. I was like a little kid playing with matches.

I liked the sound of his voice, his demeanor. He made me laugh so easily. There was definitely chemistry. He made me feel so good. I wanted to talk to him more. There was a struggle going on in me, because I knew he wasn't close to God, but I thought surely there still had to be a little sensitivity to the Lord in him. I told myself, *What could it hurt just to meet him?* I knew deep down it wouldn't be a smart move. But I hushed that still small voice.

Then, when I finally met him, I was quite overwhelmed because he was so good-looking. He dressed well, had his own business, and was a great conversationalist. It all awakened something in me. I felt more alive somehow.

It was a particularly vulnerable time in my life because my mother was dying, and my emotions were so raw. One night I came back home from visiting Mom in the hospital. I pulled into my driveway, not doing too well, and there he was, sitting on the steps to the house, waiting for me, looking like Prince Charming.

I was smitten.

We were involved for a long saga of two and a half years, much of it by phone because I was on tour. I was a little bit more of the pursuer verbally, and even physically, and now I realize how wrong that was. He wasn't showing evidence of really having God in his life, and for me God was my whole life. On top of all of this, I knew deep down he didn't truly love me. He even said to me, "Troccoli, you're bigger than life. You're too much for me. I don't want to work that hard. With you I'll have a life of challenge, and I don't want it."

Even when the writing was on the wall, I refused to see it. One time I called him at home and he had another woman at his place. I was determined to fly out there and give him an ultimatum, telling him he had to choose her or me. I remember Ellie showing up at my door. She was so concerned about me. She said, "He doesn't love you, Kathy. *He does not love you.* What are you doing?"

How could I be so dumb as not to see that the choice had already been made? But sometimes you just can't see a situation clearly when you are in the midst of it. I remember feeling helpless. A war was going on in my soul. I think I knew he didn't love me, but there was a part of me that could not fathom that as much as I felt for him, he did not feel the same way too. It reminds me of the Bonnie Raitt song "I Can't Make You Love Me." There's a line in it that says I'll close my eyes so I don't have to bear seeing the love that I know you don't feel for me.

I absolutely know now that his lack of love was God's protection, because he wasn't God's choice for me. He was not God's man. But that doesn't mean that the whole experience didn't cause enormous damage to how I felt about myself as a woman and about how attractive and desirable I could be. Yet God, as He always does, has used time and His truth to continue to heal the wounds deep in my heart.

Smoke Gets in Your Eyes

We underestimate the damage that can be done by looking for love in all the wrong places. Part of us thinks, *This is exciting, and maybe this will be it, and if it's not, at least I love the sound of it, the taste of it, the feel of it.*

Yet, when we play with fire, we get burned. Solomon asks:

Can fire be carried in the bosom without burning one's clothes? (Proverbs 6:27 NRSV)

The smoke can be the greatest danger in a fire, even more than the flame. It overcomes people, causing them to lose consciousness, or it blinds them, causing them to become disoriented, often times leading to their death. In Romans 1, Paul traces a frightening path. He talks about worshipping people instead of God. He talks about exchanging the truth of God for a lie. He talks about growing numb to what's right and wrong and even leading others down the same road. Smoke gets in our eyes. We become confused about all sorts of things. Our senses become dulled. We wander about in the dark, making ungodly choices. The results can be sexual immorality, all kinds of addictions, and becoming enslaved to our passions.

We can feel the burden in our conscience that something is wrong, but at the same time convince ourselves that the consequences won't be that bad. How much poison has spilled out by breaking a confidence? How many lives have been destroyed by flirting with a married man? How much gluttony has been released by just one taste? We are amazed, when we look back, at the tremendous cost that was exacted from us. It almost doesn't seem fair, because the initial choices seemed so small and not all that risky. *No big deal*—or so we thought.

We are so easily deceived. It is, to use another analogy, like grabbing the tail of a snake. He will turn on us, overpowering us. If we try to restrain him and put him back in his box, he will refuse to be restrained. He is a "viper," Jonathan Edwards says, who hisses and spits at God.[1]

Sometime during his middle years, Solomon grabbed the tail of a snake and it turned on him, sinking its teeth into his tender flesh and poisoning what was one of the most promising lives in all of Scripture. A sadder but wiser man, Solomon wrote the Old Testament book of Ecclesiastes as a warning to those who are tempted to look outside of God for love.

Is That All There Is?

Singer Peggy Lee was a diva from the sixties. Her song "Is That All There Is?" was a modern version of Ecclesiastes.[2] The theme of Ecclesiastes is "Vanity, vanity, all is vanity." The word *vain* or *vanity* means something passing swiftly away. Like cotton candy, it tastes good for a moment, but then it quickly disappears and we are left with the taste of grit in our mouths. Life under the sun is sweet, and we are to enjoy God's gifts of beauty, food, and sex—but none of them was ever meant to be abused. None of them was ever meant to meet our deepest needs. Philip Yancey writes:

> Ecclesiastes endures as a work of great literature and a book of great truth because it presents both sides of life on this planet: the promise of pleasures so alluring that we may devote our lives to their pursuit, and then the haunting realization that these pleasures ultimately do not satisfy. God's tantalizing world is too big for us. Made for another home, made for eternity, we finally realize that nothing this side of timeless Paradise will quiet the rumors of discontent.[3]

The first time I (Dee) read the Book of Ecclesiastes, I was confused. I thought, *This guy sounds suicidal! Why is there such a depressing book in the Bible?* But now I understand. It is a warning, a flashing red light to two groups of people:

1. To those who do not know the Lord and are trying, with things "under the sun," to fill up those places only God can fill.

2. To those who *do* know the Lord but lose that "first love" passion and then, like Solomon, try to find their way out of the wilderness. They look for love in places that will leave them lost, discouraged, and empty-handed.

Running after things "under the sun," trying to dull the ache in our hearts by eating, drinking, and being merry, concentrating on things that will pass away, whatever those may be in your life—that is the "vanity of vanities." It is the opposite of the "Song of Songs," which is setting our affections on Jesus and finding the One, and the only One, who can give unfailing love.

The authors of *The Sacred Romance* say that women, generally speaking, long for intimacy; and men, generally speaking, long for adventure.[4]

God will give us both in Him, and He is waiting to do so. Deep within each of us, as Blaise Pascal put it, is a "God-shaped vacuum." Solomon says the same thing:

> He [God] has also set eternity in the hearts of men; yet they [men and women] cannot fathom what God has done from beginning to end. (Ecclesiastes 3:11)

When I (Dee) was a young woman, I was aware of an emptiness in my life, but I could not "fathom" that the longing I had was a longing for God. Instead, I began to pursue a four-part plan:

1. Get thin and gorgeous.
2. Snare a handsome man with a bright financial future.
3. Have beautiful children.
4. Live happily ever after in an extravagant house overlooking the Pacific Ocean.

I imagined baking chocolate chip cookies (and staying thin) in my *Better Homes and Garden's* kitchen with a magnificent view of the breaking surf. After a bedtime story I would tuck my children into their Queen Anne beds, pulling log-cabin quilts gently up to their chins. Then, while the children slept sweetly, I would spend the evening with my strong and gentle husband in our library. We would read as we cuddled on our dark green leather sofa, listening to the fire crackle in the fireplace and the waves crashing on the beach.

I felt certain that when I had all this, the emptiness in my heart would be gone.

However, after I'd gotten thin, snared a man, and had a lovely little baby (the house on the Pacific was still a dream), the ache in me had actually *increased*. Life seemed so monotonous. I think the author of Ecclesiastes must have understood *laundry* and *dishes* and *bad hair days*, because he writes:

> *What has been will be again,*
> *what has been done will be done again;*
> *there is nothing new under the sun.* (Ecclesiastes 1:9)

Not only was life repetitive, it was difficult. My husband was gone all the time. As Solomon says, life is not fair, for the more powerful take advantage of the less powerful. As a medical student, Steve was on the bottom of the ladder. Therefore, I was constantly alone with our colicky baby, who screamed, it seemed, until he was three.

Ecclesiastes shows us earthly life is hard. It is especially hard for those who have blinders on, *but even faith in Jesus does not cancel out life as it really is.* That is a key lesson of Ecclesiastes, for this world is not intended to be our final home, and we are not supposed to set our affections on it. Over and over Ecclesiastes shows us the sorrow of life on earth:

> *Again I looked and saw all the oppression that was taking place under the sun:*
> *I saw the tears of the oppressed—*
> *and they have no comforter;*
> *power was on the side of their oppressors—*
> *and they have no comforter.* (Ecclesiastes 4:1–2)

Life is especially difficult when you have "no comforter." I would often lie on our bed with our wailing baby and cry with him. I never imagined motherhood would be so challenging.

One day, when I had finally gotten the baby to sleep, I came out and started folding the laundry, again. I thought: *Is this what I've been waiting for? Is life going to be a series of trivial maintenance duties punctuated by an occasional dinner out or a new outfit?* Ecclesiastes expressed my feelings perfectly:

> *So I hated life, because the work that is done under the sun was grievous to me. All of it is meaningless, a chasing after the wind.* (Ecclesiastes 2:17)

I took my frustration out on my husband, thinking, in my foolishness, that somehow my misery was his fault. One night I took a pan and threw it across the room at him and screamed, "You are not meeting my needs!"

Steve asked, "What are your needs?"

I said, "You should be able to figure that out!"

Bridge over Troubled Water

A few weeks later, on a late October day when the trees were a parade of colors, I received a phone call from my older sister, Sally. I could practically feel her joyful exuberance through the phone. With great excitement she told me:

"Dee, something wonderful has happened to me!"

"What?"

"Dee, this is too important for me not to tell you in person. Could I come to Indianapolis for a few days?"

"Please come," I pleaded. I began to cry. "I'm lonely. I feel overwhelmed. Life seems so disappointing right now."

"Dee, I understand. But I want to share with you something that will make an enormous difference."

When Sally arrived, I barely let her get her coat off. "Tell me, tell me—what has happened?"

She smiled. "I've given my life to Jesus."

I was stunned. *Jesus? This was the good news?* I could hardly believe it, but my sister had become one of those "born-agains." She pulled out her Bible and started "sharing" verses with me. When I got up to go to the kitchen to fix us some tea, she followed me, her Bible open, pestering me with questions.

"Who *do* you think Jesus is, Dee?" (I wasn't sure. So she read from the first chapter of the Gospel of John.)

"Do you understand why He came?" (I was stumped. So she read from the third chapter of the Gospel of John.)

"Do you know what He wants from you?" (No idea. So she read from the tenth chapter of the Gospel of John.)

I kept trying to change the subject. Sally kept bringing it back to Jesus. I didn't want to talk about Jesus. I didn't want to be preached at. I didn't want her following me around with the Bible. I just wanted my sister to go home. This was only the first day, and Sally planned to stay three days.

They were the three longest days of my life.

When Sally's departure day *finally* arrived, we awoke to the sound of wind and ice against the bedroom window. When we opened the drapes, we saw that snow had transformed our world. Sally's Ford Falcon was buried underneath a mound of white powder. On the radio the announcers told people the blizzard would last all day. "Stay inside," they warned in their deep radio voices. "The streets are not safe."

I thought, *The streets are not safe? I'm certainly not safe housebound with my fanatical sister!*

Let It Snow

All this, I see now, was God's mercy. Not only did He provide the blizzard, He gave Sally the wisdom and the strength to persist in talking to me.

Sally knew me. She knew things most people didn't know. She knew Steve and I had made choices that had disappointed the heart of God. She knew ways I had broken our parents' hearts. She helped me admit my sinfulness and see my need for forgiveness. Like a child having a skinned knee scrubbed, I began to cry. She came over to the sofa and put her arms around me. She said, "God promises that if you put your trust in Jesus, He will forgive you, He will cleanse you, He will make you whiter than snow."

How amazing it was at that moment to look outside my window. There was a glistening blanket covering our yard. I thought, *How wonderful it would be to be that clean.* I was listening now, for the Holy Spirit was beginning to thaw my icy heart.

My sister began to talk to me more intimately about Jesus. She said that He wanted me to love Him, know Him, and live for Him.

I liked the idea of being forgiven, of being "whiter than snow," but I wasn't sure I liked the part about giving my life over to someone else. What was living for Jesus going to mean in my life? Would I still get my house overlooking the Pacific Ocean—or might He send me to Africa to live in a snake- and spider-infested hut?

Looking back, I am thankful for my sister's honesty. Sometimes we are so eager to get people across the goal line that we fail to tell them the whole truth, as Jesus did. It is true that salvation is a free gift, but when you come to Jesus, it has to be for exactly who He is. And He is Lord.

You Made Me Love You

I (Kathy) also came to Christ as a young woman and, like Dee, met someone who was willing to tell me the truth. I met Cindy while working at a Long Island community swimming pool. I was hardly making any money singing at clubs on the weekends, so I took the day job.

Cindy would read her Bible during her lunch hour. Sometimes she'd even stay at her desk reading this big black book. Everyone, including myself, thought she was a "Jesus Freak." We thought it was so uncool to sit there and read the Bible.

It definitely impressed me, though, that she didn't care what people thought. I considered myself religious, but Cindy had something different.

I kept asking her questions, because I wondered why she was interested in something so boring. I also found it challenging to ask her questions that I knew she might not be able to answer. Every time I stumped her I felt better about what I believed to be the truth.

One day I was in my usual mode of twenty questions. I looked at Cindy as this poor naive girl who was basing her whole life and beliefs on something that was written thousands of years ago. In the middle of our banter, she sat silent for a minute and looked up at me with piercing eyes. She then said, "You know, Kath, I'm never going to be able to answer all of your questions, but one thing I'm certain of: Jesus will be Lord whether you ever accept Him or not."

Boom. The truth hit me right between the eyes. I began to see.

A Candle in the Wind

The tragic life and death of Marilyn Monroe inspired the song "A Candle in the Wind." Though blessed with beauty, fame, wealth, and popularity, she seemed like a little girl lost and never found the love for which she longed. Her quiet desperation led to a tragic end.

Elton John sang the song again after the death of Princess Diana. Here was this lovely woman whose face graced the covers of thousands of magazines. She evidenced compassion, was a devoted mother, and affected many lives for the good. Millions of people loved and admired her.

Even so, Diana often spoke about wanting to know true love and true happiness. In the midst of this searching, her life was snuffed out like a candle in the wind.

We are in a battle for our souls. It is important to realize that all of us wrestle, not against flesh and blood, but against powers and principalities. Satan blows smoke in our eyes, hoping to keep us disoriented. He is even successful, at times, in encouraging a premature death. For persisting in the wrong paths, whether from wickedness or foolishness, can lead to destructive behaviors such as alcoholism, running with the wrong crowd, and thrill-seeking stunts. Solomon warns:

> Do not be overwicked,
> and do not be a fool—
> why die before your time? (Ecclesiastes 7:17)

Though we didn't know it, after the truth had been shared with each of us, we entered a battlefield. The enemy had been provoked. He sought ways to destroy our newly built fortresses of truth.

I (Kathy) struggled with the reactions of my family and friends. Some of them thought I was joining a cult. Some feminist friends of mine thought I was retreating to the days when women had no say, no vote, and no identity.

But Jesus was wooing me. I couldn't deny His life and the things that were being told to me. If He was the truth and I refused Him, I might be refusing the greatest gift of my life.

I (Dee) struggled for a whole month after my sister left. If Jesus led me somewhere other than to my dream house on the Pacific Ocean, would I experience fulfillment? Would I find the happiness for which I longed?

Sally left behind a modern paraphrase of the New Testament by J. B. Phillips. She knew I needed intellectual reasons for believing in Christ, so she gave me *Mere Christianity* by C. S. Lewis. She also knew I needed to understand intimacy with Christ, so she gave me *The Cross and the Switchblade* by David Wilkerson. I devoured both books. Lewis persuaded me of the rationality of Christianity, but it was Wilkerson who thrilled my heart. He followed a God who bent down and answered prayer, who led him, specifically, each day. Could it be?

Was it possible that God could be as personal, as mindful of me, as Wilkerson had experienced? Would He really love me like that?

Just in Time

Both Kathy and I were haunted by the same question: Had we been created for a deeper love than the world had to offer?

We were definitely beginning to have a healthy fear of the Lord, which Solomon says is "the beginning of wisdom."

On a November day in 1966, I (Dee) knelt, broken before God. And twelve years later, I (Kathy) realized my desperate need and surrendered my life to Christ as well.

Many of the haunting questions of Ecclesiastes, questions we harbored in our hearts as we were wrestling with the Holy Spirit, were answered the day we yielded our lives to Jesus. The light of Christ shone down on us, and the darkness was dispelled:

Solomon cried: There is nothing new under the sun!

Yet that day, Jesus made each of us *new*. He changed our hearts, our perspectives, our purpose in life. We saw our sin, we wept, and we were cleansed. Each of us was a *new* creation.

Solomon lamented: This world is full of trouble! I've seen the tears of the oppressed!

Though receiving Christ did not remove trouble from our lives, now there was a huge difference. Though Jesus said, "In this world you will have trouble," He also said, "But take heart! I have overcome the world" (John 16:33). God began to fill our lives with the strength to live in an unfair world.

Solomon despaired: I hate the things for which I have toiled, because I cannot take them with me when I die. I feel like I've been chasing the wind.

Jesus helped us understand that *that* was why we should not lay up for ourselves things on earth, but instead, lay up for ourselves things in heaven. For Dee, building a house overlooking the ocean seemed less crucial somehow, for she wanted to own something of eternal value, something that would not pass away. Kathy found a deep desire to affect the eternal in peoples' lives.

Solomon doubted: Is there anything after death? How do I know that my spirit will live on?

Jesus couldn't have been clearer. He said: "I am the resurrection and the life. He who believes in me will live, even though he dies" (John 11:25). God's Spirit bore witness with our spirits that we had been given eternal life, and that it had already begun.

Yet Ecclesiastes was not written as a warning primarily to the unbeliever (though the same truth applies) but to the believer. As vital as salvation is, it is just the beginning of our life.

When we focus only on salvation, we are like the couple who spends an enormous amount of money and time on the *wedding* but neglects the *marriage*.

That's exactly what happened to Solomon. After his beginning years with the Lord when God blessed Solomon with wisdom, wealth, fame, and the peace of His presence, Solomon coasted. He neglected his "marriage" to the Lord.

Lady in Red

In *The King and I*, the king of Siam says men are like bees and women are like flowers. Bees can gather nectar from many flowers, but flowers must not ever fly from bee to bee to bee! Unfortunately, that was generally the thinking of kings of the Old Testament. They collected harems, not only for sexual pleasure, but to increase their political clout. (Marrying the daughter of a foreign leader increased their influence with that leader.) Yet God had clearly commanded Solomon:

> *You must not intermarry with them, because they will surely turn your hearts after their gods.* (1 Kings 11:2)

When Solomon was young, he obeyed. But then he took his relationship with the Lord for granted. Lovely women in beaded bodices or silky red kimonos, young women from all tribes and nations, came sauntering through the door he had foolishly left open. Before long King Solomon

> *loved many foreign women besides Pharaoh's daughter—Moabites, Ammonites, Edomites, Sidonians and Hittites. . . . Solomon held fast to them in love. He had seven hundred wives of royal birth and three hundred concubines, and his wives led him astray.* (1 Kings 11:1–3)

When Solomon said, "Honey, you are one in a thousand," he meant it! God didn't wink and look the other way.

The LORD became angry with Solomon because his heart had turned away from the LORD, the God of Israel, who had appeared to him twice. (1 Kings 11:9)

God took the kingdom from Solomon, and Solomon never really recovered. He lost the joy, the peace, and the privilege of serving the Lord.

We scratch our heads, thinking, *Solomon! How could you have been so dense?* Solomon agreed. From his experiences he wrote the Book of Ecclesiastes to warn us of what will happen if we are not diligent in keeping our love relationship with the Lord alive.

Why, after Solomon had known the sweetness of fellowship with the Lord, did he go back to looking for love in all the wrong places? Why do any of us?

Are You Lonesome Tonight?

What I (Kathy) sense in myself and what I've sensed as I've talked to believers on the road is that we get impatient. We don't feel like there is enough immediate payback. We're lonely, we may be facing some kind of wilderness experience, and we don't want to wait for God to fill our needs. So we settle for a temporary filling. I have a friend who has recently left a homosexual lifestyle. She said, "I've got to tell you, I miss the high. I miss the camaraderie. I miss the titillation of it." My friend has stayed pure because she's hanging on to God and His promises, and she knows if she returns to her old life it is just going to be a quick fix with a false peace and then all will come crashing down. But it can be lonely waiting on God. It's like the Lazarus story. Jesus stayed where He was for two days, and Mary and Martha were thinking, *Are You there? Do You care?*

Yet nothing in my life is worth the cost of sacrificing the peace of God. The partying, the sizzle, the chemistry—it's all so attractive, but none of it is worth the sacrifice of God's peace. Is it fun? It can be. Does it give pleasure? Absolutely. But I don't know anyone, including myself, who doesn't awaken after engaging in worldly pleasure to a feeling of emptiness, to the sad realization that the peace of God has slipped away. In the moment, it makes you feel alive. But it's that false aliveness, that false sense of passion, that false sense of euphoria.

Satan encourages us not to stop and think. He says, "Come on, it's great, don't miss it." We finally give in and say, "Okay . . ." And then, *Boom!* He runs off and you're left with a pile of shame and guilt. You get close to the fire, then you enter the fire and find yourself trying to do the Flintstones back-pedal. I say it because I've lived it. I've crossed some lines. I've played with fire. I realize now it's all such death, and it breeds death. I want the peace of God more than anything. Sometimes in the peace of God you can feel a little lonely, but that's okay.

We shake our heads in amazement at the Israelites, who built and worshipped a gold idol right after God had parted the Red Sea and led them through. Why couldn't they trust Him? Why couldn't they wait for Moses to come down from the mountain? Couldn't they see how foolish they were being? Yet we do the same thing. When God does not immediately deliver us, we may drive, in a kind of panic, to the mall, hoping a new outfit will deliver us from the boredom; or we may open the freezer door, down the Rocky Road, hoping to ease the stress; or we may run to the familiar arms of a secret sin, the adulterous lover we thought we had left behind, thinking that secret sin will fill the chasm of loneliness in our heart. But, like the Israelites, instead of finding deliverance, we find ourselves returning to slavery, to emptiness, and to futility. And then we cry, with Solomon, "Meaningless, meaningless—my life is meaningless."

All of the things "under the sun" can give us a temporary high, a faster fix than waiting upon God. But that high never, ever lasts. That's exactly what happened to Solomon, and he describes it beautifully in Ecclesiastes. He was a believer when he went looking for love. When life became difficult, instead of waiting on God, he began building a palace and a harem. He said:

I denied myself nothing my eyes desired;
I refused my heart no pleasure. (Ecclesiastes 2:10a)

And though he found some delight in this, at the end of the day:

When I surveyed all that my hands had done
and what I had toiled to achieve,
everything was meaningless, a chasing after the wind;
nothing was gained under the sun. (Ecclesiastes 2:11)

Though he knew the Lord, Solomon wasted his life. He gave up being able to have an eternal impact on peoples' lives, he gave up the comfort of having God's peace in his heart, and he gave up truly knowing a joy unspeakable. He traded them all for transitory pleasures. And all of those years of pleasure were simply gone with the wind.

Blowing in the Wind

Margaret Mitchell was a young author when she was killed by a runaway horse and carriage, but the book she left behind won the Pulitzer Prize and was called the romance of the century. At first MGM Studios was hesitant to make it into a movie, claiming that "no Civil War picture ever made a dime."[5] But as the book's sales soared, MGM took a risk, and *Gone with the Wind* became the blockbuster of blockbusters. Why?

The story haunts us. It is a story of destruction; of the old South destroyed because it clung to slavery; of Scarlett O'Hara wrecking many lives, including her own, by running after her best friend's husband. As Solomon warned, we will "inherit the wind" if we persist in wrong choices.

What Kind of Fool Am I?

How could beautiful, bewitching Scarlett O'Hara be so foolish as to throw herself at spineless, sad-eyed, and delicate Ashley Wilkes? How could she spurn the dashing and daring Rhett Butler, a man with such smoldering sex appeal? Throughout the story we keep waiting for Scarlett to come to her senses. How could she keep chasing Ashley when a man like Rhett was waiting in the wings?

Rhett loved Scarlett. It was he who rescued her, again and again, but she didn't appreciate that. He understood her, and he loved her even in her weakness—treating her gently, like the child that she was. As God is both Husband and Father to us, Rhett was to Scarlett—loving her passionately yet also understanding her and giving her mercy, the way a father might a child.

This is how God is portrayed in the Book of Hosea. He loves us tenderly, like a father, and longs for fidelity from us, like a husband. Listen to His heartbreak:

> *It was I who taught Ephraim to walk,*
> *taking them by the arms;*
> *but they did not realize*
> *it was I who healed them.*
> *I led them with cords of human kindness,*
> *with ties of love;*
> *I lifted the yoke from their neck*
> *and bent down to feed them.*
> *How can I give you up, Ephraim?*
> *How can I hand you over, Israel?* (Hosea 11:3–4, 8)

Far too often, we have not acknowledged the kindness of the Lord. He makes available to us all that we need in this life, but we scurry about longing to be satisfied, as if God is not aware of our needs. We are like Scarlett. Rhett tried to warn her, saying, "I feel sorry for you, Scarlett. You are throwing away love with both hands and grabbing for that which will never love you."[6]

At the close of the story, when Scarlett finally realizes what she has thrown away, she runs home to Rhett, her dark hair flying, her dress splattered with mud, thinking:

I love him. . . . And if it hadn't been for Ashley, I'd have realized it long ago. I've never been able to see the world at all, because Ashley stood in the way. . . . Rhett has never let me down. . . . He's loved me all along and I've been so mean to him. Time and again, I've hurt him. . . . I'll tell him everything. . . . He'll understand. He's always understood.[7]

That's how it can be with us. As long as we try to let someone or something else fill the void in our life, we keep Jesus out, blocking the flow of His love. We don't realize what He has done for us, how He has cared for us, how He longs to meet our deepest needs each and every day.

Realizing that Ashley would never meet her needs, Scarlett comes to her senses. She frantically runs home to Rhett. She finds him sitting alone, slumped in a chair, seemingly lifeless, a decanter on the table. She goes on and on, confessing her love, pleading, and begging for forgiveness. He wearily responds:

I loved you. . . . I thought Ashley would fade out of your mind. . . . I tried everything I knew and nothing worked. And I loved you so, Scarlett. If you had only let me, I could have loved you as gently and as tenderly as ever a man loved a woman.

Scarlett cries, desperately:

Darling, I'm so sorry but I'll make it all up to you! We can be so happy, now that we know the truth and—Rhett—look at me, Rhett! . . . Rhett, if you once loved me so much, there must be something left for me! . . . You don't love me any more? . . . I love you![8]

The readers and the moviegoers are breathless. Is it too late? Will Rhett once again sweep Scarlett into his strong arms? Will all be forgiven? Will there be a happy ending?

Hollywood permitted the first swearword in a movie to come from Rhett's lips when he turned to her and said:

Frankly, my dear, I don't give a damn.[9]

Fortunately for us, this is where the parallel ends.

For though human love grows faint and runs dry, God is always faithful. In our humanness, rejection closes us down and causes us to walk away. But God, in His holiness, leaves the door open and walks toward us. He doesn't hold our times of adultery against us. We surely may live through the consequences of our choices, but God will always bring us back into a new beginning. Whenever we sincerely confess our sin, whenever we truly take the steps back to Him, He welcomes us with open arms, longing to continue His romance with us.

Stubborn Love

The Lord commanded Hosea to keep showing love to his unfaithful wife. Why? To paint a picture for each of us, His unfaithful brides:

> *Go, show your love to your wife again, though she is loved by another and is an adulteress. Love her as the* LORD *loves the Israelites, though they turn to other gods and love the sacred raisin cakes.* (Hosea 3:1)

It's His stubborn love that simply will not let go of us. Mary Blye Howe, in the *Dallas Morning News*, said that while all metaphors of God are helpful, the metaphor of God as a Bridegroom, as a Lover, is unique:

> Romantic love encompasses characteristics that no other love includes. A lover leaves all others and "cleaves" to the soul with whom he is united. He feels anguish and a sense of incompleteness in the other's absence.

Do you understand that God longs for intimacy with you? He made you for Himself. Howe continues:

God is a being that thirsts for us individually . . . who will stop at nothing to gain our love in return. Like a lover, God sees each of us as
uniquely beautiful. Lovers are consumed by desire, wanting just to be
near another. They lie awake thinking of the one they love, examining
new ideas that might win their love, counting the days when they'll be
near that person again. . . . How lovely![10]

Do you remember how the Lord courted you? Do you remember that
sweet season when you first encountered the love of Jesus?

ACT I

First Love

❧

Orchestra
allegro scherzando
(Begin briskly, keeping the tempo lively
and the spirit cheerful)

4

It Had to Be You

I (KATHY) HAVE BEEN TRAVELING FOR MANY YEARS. MY CONCERTS and speaking engagements take me to places all over the world. Sometimes they are as dull as a row of fast-food restaurants in Nowhere, USA, but sometimes they are as exciting as dining at a fine restaurant with the best view of the sun setting over the Caribbean. It is in these lovely far-away places that the fire in me to share my life with someone still burns with a passionate flame:

January 29, 1995

It's my second night of the "Forever Friends" cruise. Sandi Patty has been gracious enough to ask me to go a second year. It's absolutely lovely here. The crystal blue water, the bright warm sun—I'm far away from the winter in New York.

Every time I experience anything like this—I think about you—and yearn to be with you—I long to make memories with you.

You're somewhere in the world tonight.

I miss you.

January 19, 1996

French toast . . . coffee . . . On a balcony this morning—overlooking the ocean . . . Cancún, Mexico. I am overwhelmed by some of the amazing things I get to experience because God has given me a voice.

Of course, as you know by now, there are never these kinds of moments when my thoughts don't turn to you.

To share this with you someday: walking along the beach hand in hand, hearing the serenade of the waves, breathing in the fresh night air as the sun sets gently on the horizon— ah . . . the romance of it all . . .

When I (Dee) first read these entries, I was struck by the parallel of Kathy's yearning and the yearning that God has for each of us. He wants us to be so close to Him. Kathy told me, "It's such a sweet thought to think that God could be lonely for me."

It can seem difficult to believe that He really does yearn for us. He is so great, and we are so small. He is so holy, and we are so unholy. But just as we are relational, so is the One in whose image we are made. God doesn't need anything, but He does want our love and devotion. When did He begin to dream of a relationship with us?

Long before he laid down earth's foundations, he had us in mind, had settled on us as the focus of his love, to be made whole and holy by his love. Long, long ago he decided to adopt us into his family through Jesus Christ. (What pleasure he took in planning this!) (Ephesians 1:4–5 MSG)

God is the pursuer. He is lonely for us. He is the Bridegroom longing for His Bride.

It is a mystery, and yet God created earthly bridegrooms to foreshadow the ultimate Bridegroom. Men are told to provide for their wives, love their wives, and sacrifice for their wives. When Kathy sees that kindness in men, it makes her lonely for the man of her dreams:

September 30, 1995

I've been on the road so much . . . traveling through Washington today with 4 Him and Clay Crosse . . . These guys have been so good and kind to me. I guess it makes me miss you even more . . .

The weather has that cool fall touch to it. Such a beautiful time of year.

I long for you, a home, and a fireplace.

When chaste young couples daydream of their future together, they anticipate the time when they will no longer have to part at night, each going to their own lonely beds. They dream of going home together, whether it is to a studio apartment or a colonial estate. Finally, they will be husband and wife.

Each summer evening before their wedding day, our daughter Sally and her future husband would linger at our cottage, not wanting to part. The angst was palpable. But each night, they would encourage each other by reminding themselves that soon, and very soon, they would be going home *together.*

I'll Go Home with Bonnie Jean!

In the Scottish musical *Brigadoon,* the future bridegroom pines for the day when he will be able to take his bride, Bonnie Jean, home. He imagines how wonderful it will be to wake up in the morning with her, to plan their day, and to sit by the evening fire together. He tells his friends of the home he is preparing, and of how excited he is to take her there. Anticipating that time with great joy, he dances, along with the whole village, to "I'll Go Home with Bonnie Jean!"

It is a precious thought to think that Jesus, our Bridegroom, is preparing a place for us, looking forward to the time when He will come and take us home. We feel sure that He hopes we are also anticipating this day. For what bridegroom wants an apathetic bride?

Missing You

When I (Kathy) was looking for songs for my *Sounds of Heaven* record, my manager, the record company, and I listened to a tape by Chris Rice. (He wrote "Go Light Your World" and "Hallelujahs.") At that time he was a fairly unknown singer and songwriter, but I was so taken with his music. He has a way of writing lyrics that pierce my heart. Many of them express the longing I have to be close to Jesus. Chris's tape was simple, with just Chris and his guitar. The last song was called "Missing You." It didn't have a dramatic commercial-type chorus in which you recognize, *Wow, that's a hit song.* But, oh, how it touched me.

> I heard about the day You went away
> You said You had to go prepare a place
> And even though I've never seen Your face
> I'm missing You
>
> I lie awake tonight and watch the sky
> And I wish it didn't have to be so high
> 'Cause I'm belonging on the other side
> And I'm missing You

I put my head down as I listened to the lyrics. I found myself weeping. When the song was over, I looked up and realized that I was the only one who had been touched so deeply. I think that's because a single person has a little more opportunity to have a longing and an ache for intimacy than does a person in a good marriage. I can't cuddle at night, nor can I have that sense of belonging when I turn out the lights that married people can. So, yes, I do miss Jesus. I long for Him to come and sweep me into His arms, far beyond this world.

Somewhere over the Rainbow

In biblical times, the Jewish marriage ceremony had three distinct parts. The first was the betrothal, as in the betrothal of Mary and Joseph. After the betrothal, the woman was considered the man's bride. It was a permanent and legally binding commitment, though the marriage had not been consummated.

Following this, there was a period of separation during which the bridegroom prepared for the bride to come and live with him. He would actually add a room to his father's house for his new wife and himself.

Then, when the *bridegroom's father* felt all was ready, the bridegroom would come, in a great processional, for the bride. In his youth, Solomon was close to the Lord and provides a picture of our ultimate Bridegroom. He is betrothed to the Shulammite maiden, but then he goes away, to prepare a place. He comes back for her, and this scene gives us a glimpse of the majesty of the processional that will occur when Christ comes back for us:

> *Who is this coming up from the desert*
> *like a column of smoke,*
> *perfumed with myrrh and incense*
> *made from all the spices of the merchant?*
> *Look! It is Solomon's carriage,*
> *escorted by sixty warriors. . . .*
> *Come out, you daughters of Zion,*
> *and look at King Solomon wearing the crown,*
> *the crown with which his mother crowned him*
> *on the day of his wedding,*
> *the day his heart rejoiced.* (Song of Songs 3:6–7, 11)

The bride didn't know when the bridegroom would come for her, so she needed to be ready. When he came, the last part of the ceremony was performed, a seven-day celebration including a great wedding feast. It was after this that the bridegroom finally took his bride home.

This makes the picture Jesus paints particularly meaningful. We are betrothed to Him. We are His Bride, but we are in the period of separation. He is preparing a place for us. Jesus said:

> *In my Father's house are many rooms; if it were not so, I would have told you. I am going there to prepare a place for you. And if I go and prepare a place for you, I will come back and take you to be with me.* (John 14:2–3)

When Jesus comes, it will be in the greatest processional of all. And He will take us away, far above this world. Our finite minds cannot fathom the place He is preparing. But we do know we will live forever without shedding a tear, we do know we will have eternal peace, and best of all, we do know we will be with Jesus face to face. We will be reunited with loved ones. There will be harmony, security, and the sweet comfort of family and friends.

November 29, 1996

What a peaceful Thanksgiving this has been. Pamela flew in, Jen and the kids are here. All of Ellie and Frank's family are here—Just came back from Mt. Vernon (George Washington's house) . . . ate at Old Town . . . it's freezing cold . . . lots of hugs and snuggling today. I love when my precious nieces Maria and Gina wrap their arms around me—my prayers that I would grow closer to them have come to pass—I love them so much . . . Time off is wonderful—To wake up and have nothing to do but enjoy life, relax, etc., is priceless to me.

Of course at this time of year I think of you more every day—I can't enter into the warmth and romance of it all

without the thought that one day you might be here—that
you'd buy me something in the Old Christmas store I was
just in—that you'd put your arm around me and draw me
close as we walk through the cold—that I would smile at you
and you would know how in love I am with you—and that
even though the day would be rich and full—my highlight
would be to be in your arms through the night.

We will be His Bride. We will smile at Him and He will draw us close. We will know how much He loves us. And He will take us home, and hold us, all through the night.

I'll Be Your Shelter

Though all grooms, of course, fall short of the holiness of Christ, they give us a glimpse of the ultimate Bridegroom. The Old Testament often gives us a "Christ figure" to help us faintly see our awesome God. Moses was a deliverer, David a shepherd-king, Melchizedek a priest. We are also given three bridegrooms, so that we might glimpse the wonder of our ultimate Bridegroom. Hosea, Solomon, and Boaz, though they all had human frailties, still show us an aspect of Christ the Bridegroom.

Hosea was a faithful husband, though his adulterous bride broke his heart again and again. Though our love for God is "like the morning mist, like the early dew that disappears" (Hosea 6:4b), His love for us is steadfast and true:

> As surely as the sun rises,
>   he will appear;
> he will come to us like the winter rains,
>   like the spring rains that water the earth. (Hosea 6:3b)

Solomon, in the Song of Songs, gives us a glimpse of how much our God adores us, of how He yearns for our love:

How delightful is your love, my sister, my bride!
How much more pleasing is your love than wine,
and the fragrance of your perfume than any spice! (Song of Songs 4:10)

And in the Book of Ruth, Boaz was a "kinsman-redeemer" who rescued and redeemed his bride, Ruth. I (Dee) treasure the Book of Ruth and found in it much inspiration for my book *The Friendships of Women*. But this time, instead of looking at it from the perspective of friendship, I have looked at the romance in the book, the wonderful love story between Boaz and Ruth.

Sometimes the people in the Bible seem so *ancient* that it is hard to imagine they really lived, loved, and laughed. I have a friend who is in many ways a contemporary Ruth. Jill's love story has brought the romance and the people in the Book of Ruth alive to me.

Jill and her husband, Russ Wolford, had a farm on the outskirts of town. In a little white farmhouse lived, truly, a joyful mother, a loving father, and their four precious children. Yet tragedy lurked around the corner, for Russ was to be killed in a farming accident in his thirties. The year before it happened, Russ promised the children a trip to Disneyland if they gave up television for twelve entire months. Jill said, "Looking back, I'm truly thankful for that year. The absence of television led to popcorn and games by the fire; bike rides and picnics in the country; snuggling on the couch with good books, good conversation, and so much laughter."

The laughter ceased on a summer day when Russ lifted an irrigation pipe high in the air. It struck a live electrical wire.

I'll never, ever forget visiting Jill in her white farmhouse after the funeral. She was so thin, so pale. She wept as she told me: "The children aren't sleeping. They have nightmares about their dad. They're also afraid we'll have to move. Dee, please pray we don't lose the farm. They've lost so much already—I don't want them to leave the only home they've ever known." As I traveled back to my house that day, I was sobbing, praying God would have mercy on them.

But they ended up losing their home. They had to move into town. Like Ruth, Jill lost her husband, lost her land, and lost her home.

Two years later, at Christmas, I stopped by with a plate of cookies. Jill's radiance made me inquisitive. "Jill, you are glowing. Why?"

She blushed. "Oh, Dee. His name is Keith Johnson, and he is so wonderful, so godly. He absolutely adores the children. He says we are the family for which he has always longed. He's handsome, he's kind, and he's a farmer!"

Keith Johnson married Jill, sold his own property in order to redeem Jill's rented farm, moved the family back home, and erected a huge sign that read:

The Wolford-Johnsons

Keith is Jill's Boaz, a contemporary kinsman-redeemer.

Ruth and Naomi were bereft of their husbands, bereft of their land, and bereft of their home. Women in ancient Israel could not own property. Essentially, they were homeless. But God provided a law, "the law of the kinsman-redeemer," for the benefit of the widow. If her late husband had a brother, or a kinsman, then that relative had a responsibility to the widow. He was to redeem the property and, if possible, marry the widow and raise the first son in the late kinsman's name. This way the family name would not be blotted out.

When the Jews read the Book of Ruth, they read about the heartache of Naomi and Ruth in the opening chapter. It begins with a famine and is followed by continuing devastation to both of these women.

But by the second chapter, the women have returned to Bethlehem, the barley harvest is beginning, and you can almost hear the violins begin to play:

Now Naomi had a relative on her husband's side, from the clan of Elimelech, a man of standing, whose name was Boaz. (Ruth 2:1)

Clearly, romance waited in the wings. We are breathless. Will the prince find the princess?

Another Jewish law allowed widows and strangers to glean in the fields, picking up leftover grain. Out of hundreds of fields in Bethlehem, Ruth "happens" into the field of Boaz. When Boaz arrives to check on his harvesters, he notices this lovely young woman immediately. He is curious, inquires about her, and receives a glowing report.

Can't you just picture this masculine man calling Ruth over? I imagine his voice was deep, his eyes, kind:

> My daughter, listen to me. Don't go and glean in another field and don't go away from here. Stay here with my servant girls. Watch the field where the men are harvesting, and follow along after the girls. I have told the men not to touch you. And whenever you are thirsty, go and get a drink from the water jars the men have filled. (Ruth 2:8–9)

Ruth is overwhelmed at Boaz's tender mercy, the way we feel when we are first aware of the tender mercy of the Lord. She bows down to the ground and exclaims:

> Why have I found such favor in your eyes that you notice me—a foreigner? (Ruth 2:10b)

Just as the Shulammite maiden protested, "Do not stare at me because I am dark," Ruth cannot imagine why Boaz would be interested in her. But he is. He is on a quest for her love.

Boaz is a shelter for Ruth, a haven. He knows her self-esteem is fragile, and he sensitively goes out of his way to protect her. He takes the harvesters aside and tells them:

> Even if she gathers among the sheaves, don't embarrass her. Rather, pull out some stalks for her from the bundles and leave them for her to pick up, and don't rebuke her. (Ruth 2:15–16)

What a guy! How we love to be treated so tenderly by men.

January 29, 2000

If I had not fallen in love with you, Lord, I would probably be a militant feminist . . . You've brought me so much balance—each year you teach me more and more about what it means to be your woman, while you allow me to get glimpses of your heart in some of the men that cross my path . . .

Much to my surprise I've arrived at a place of loving and even yearning for chivalry . . . I feel like royalty when a door is held open for me, when a chair is pushed back for me, and when a hand reaches to help me out of a car.

I pray that I will know in this life what it means to be treated like a princess by a man whom you have called to be my prince.

When we meet men who pray passionately, who walk in the fear of a holy God, who continually choose the highest path, who radiate His love and, yes, His chivalry, we catch a glimpse of Jesus. *Truly* godly men (and they are rare) are so different from most men. They are interested in you, they are great listeners, and they are gifted in intimacy. Today Hollywood would probably never capture the meaning of the Book of Ruth. They'd likely add immorality to the story. They'd miss its beautiful symbolism. And they'd have difficulty grasping that the magnetism and charisma of Boaz came from his deep connection to God.

Boaz exhibits such tenderness, such strength, such chivalry. Nearly every word out of his mouth is a prayer. He affirms Ruth, understands her loneliness, and prays diligently for her:

> *I've been told all about what you have done for your mother-in-law since the death of your husband—how you left your father and mother and your homeland and came to live with a people you did not know before. May the LORD repay you for what you have done. May you be richly rewarded by the LORD, the God of Israel, under whose wings you have come to take refuge.* (Ruth 2:11–12)

Just as every bridegroom is meant to be a foreshadowing of the ultimate Bridegroom, every bride, from the beginning of time, was meant to be a foreshadowing of the ultimate Bride, the invisible Church, the Bride of Christ.

My Girl

Eve, the first bride, was breathtakingly beautiful to Adam. When he saw her, he knew. She was his completion. Though both Adam and Eve were made in the image of God, they were different; they were male and female. Elisabeth Elliot writes:

> God might have given Adam another man to be his friend, to walk and talk and argue with if that was his pleasure. But Adam needed more.[1]

In *The Divine Romance,* Gene Edwards tells the story of the formation of the first bride (Eve) and the last bride (the Bride of Christ). Edwards notes some intriguing parallels:

- As Adam was lonely for Eve, God is lonely for us.

- As Adam was ecstatic when he saw Eve, God is looking forward, with great anticipation, to the completion of His holy Bride.

- As Eve reflected the nature of Adam, so the Bride of Christ is to reflect the nature of Christ.[2]

God understands loneliness. He looked at Adam and said, "It is not good for the man to be alone" (Genesis 2:18). When He fashioned Eve during Adam's sleep and then brought her to him, Adam's yearning was fulfilled and his reaction was unbounded joy.

Christopher Wordsworth (1807–1885) comments on how God formed both brides during the sleep of the bridegroom:

While Christ, the Second Adam . . . was sleeping in death on the cross, God formed for him, in his death, and by his death—even by the life-giving streams flowing from his own precious side,—the Church, the spiritual Eve, the Mother of all living; and gave her to him as his bride.[3]

Each member of that Bride is precious to the Lord. Each is known. Eve, Ruth, Mary of Bethany, you, me . . . God called each one to Himself. If you have put your trust in Christ, you have gone through the first part of the ceremony. You are His Betrothed, and you are His Bride. But now you are in the period of separation, and you are preparing for His return, for the final part of the ceremony.

The Way You Look Tonight

Jewish brides made elaborate wedding gowns during this time, desiring to be breathtaking when their groom arrived. Our wedding gowns are our characters: our purity and radiance, our integrity, and our growing devotion to Him. His Spirit helps us to prepare for the appearance of our Bridegroom.

> *Those who look to him are radiant;*
> *their faces are never covered with shame.* (Psalm 34:5)

His loving hand is molding us:

> As the form of Eve grew up in silence and secrecy under the fashioning hand of the Maker, so at this hour is the Bride being fashioned for the Lord Jesus.[4]

He knew you would be His. Before the foundation of the world, He knew. When He knit you together in your mother's womb, He knew. When you were a little child, He knew. He began wooing you.

Come to Me, Bend to Me

On the morning of his wedding day in *Brigadoon,* the bridegroom is overwhelmed with longing. As he wanders outside in the heather on the hills, he sings the hauntingly lovely "Come to Me, Bend to Me." His bride hears his song drift through her window as she prepares to put on her bridal dress. She dances in her lace camisole, reaching lithe and graceful arms toward the sound of her bridegroom's voice.

I (Dee) could hardly believe they cut "Come to Me, Bend to Me" from the movie version starring Gene Kelly. But the wedding day came, and the wedding itself, and there was no "Come to Me, Bend to Me." I went into denial, rewinding the tape, searching for the ballet. It wasn't there. I said to Steve, "I am so disappointed that they cut that song."

Dryly Steve said, "Me too. Just devastated."

They must have had a male producer, I thought. *No woman would have cut it.*

Even now when I am all alone I listen to the original score and I dance, imagining that Jesus is calling, "Come to Me, bend to Me . . ."

Jesus woos us, then He wins us, and finally, finally, He weds us.

Arise, My Love

Jesus has been thinking of us from the beginning of time. He is our Prince Charming who wants to awaken us from the spell of the wicked queen, from deathly sleep, so that we will yearn for Him as well.

Shortly before Christmas 1996, Kathy wrote in her journal:

December 12, 1996

I long to be awakened. I long to be touched in a place in my soul that I know God intended . . . I long to feel the inexpressible joy that comes from a woman in love. I long to be a bride.

Please find me.

Do you realize that Jesus has been wooing you, longing to awaken you to Him, from the time you were a little girl?

Our first awareness that Someone wonderful woos us usually occurs through His creation.

Can You Feel the Love Tonight?

When I (Kathy) was three, our family moved from Brooklyn to Long Island, which has some lovely wooded areas. I remember running around with my cousins on summer nights beneath a midnight blue-black sky. I'd be perspiring then suddenly feel the cool tinge of the New York night on my face. (I can almost smell the air as I write this.) I'd lift my eyes to the stars in the clear sky and think, just for a moment, *There's Someone bigger than me out there.*

I was so taken with the moon and the stars, I dreamed of being the first female astronaut. I talked about it so much that my mother sent away for an astronaut suit. I thought it was the coolest. It was gray silver and had a helmet that opened. I dreamed about what it would be like to fly up there—and I wondered just how far the universe went. God was wooing me, as a little girl, through the wonder of the heavens.

Author Leisha Joseph has memories of God wooing her from the time she was a little girl, memories that helped her survive so much, including a brutal rape. In *Little Girl Lost,* she tells of how God first wooed her.

When I was small, my favorite place to hide was in a thick patch of grass that was taller and deeper green than the rest of my daddy's lawn. I used to bury my face in the tender blades and deeply breathe the sweet smell of summer. I'd pull up a long blade by the roots and chew the sweet white part, lie back and look at the sky.

From my vantage point, the sky stretched forever and beyond. Gigantic billowing clouds floated by like vast schooners sailing across a sea of blue. . . .

From out of nowhere the thought came to me, I'll bet there's a God. There must be, look at all this.[5]

For Brent Curtis, one of the authors of *The Sacred Romance,* it happened, also, on summer evenings. Curtis grew up on 120 acres of New Jersey farmland. As a barefoot boy of six or seven, he would squat down on his heels in the moonlight at the edge of the creek lining the farm and listen to the music of the crickets, katydids, and cicadas.

I remember being in that place until the music of life would fill me with the knowledge of some Romance to be lived . . . the magic assured me of loves and lovers and adventures to be joined and mystery to be pursued.[6]

Do you remember how God wooed you through His creation?

God demonstrates this tenderness not only through His creation but also through the testimony of others. God brings them across our paths and prompts them to tell us their stories.

That's the Story of Love

Dee's sister Sally was wooed through the story of a freshman student at Iowa State. Sally was teaching Spanish and gave an assignment to her class to write an essay on who their best friend was and why. A freshman student named Bonnie wrote about Jesus, about how much she loved Him because He had given her life. The fragrance of Christ was released to Sally, who, consequently, put her trust in Him. Then that fragrance was released to Dee and to countless others in her path.

If we are open, the fragrance of the testimony of others is the fragrance of life. But if we are closed, their fragrance seems like the fragrance of death, because that is what we have chosen by rejecting the only name under heaven by which we can be saved. Read Paul's words carefully:

But thanks be to God, who always leads us in triumphal procession in Christ
and through us spreads everywhere the fragrance of the knowledge of him.
For we are to God the aroma of Christ among those who are being saved and
those who are perishing. To the one we are the smell of death; to the other,
the fragrance of life. (2 Corinthians 2:14–16)

Cindy released the fragrance of Christ to me (Kathy) during the summer of 1978 and had no idea how that would impact the world. At my very first *Time Out for Women* conference, I shared how I had been wooed through her testimony. I said, "Cindy was an ordinary girl with an extraordinary God. She has affected thousands of you because she affected me." Then I said, from the stage, "Cindy, I heard you might be here. Are you here?" I waited a little while but nobody came forward. There were ten thousand women there and they began to laugh nervously.

But then, all of a sudden, Cindy came running through the doors from the overflow room. She ran right onto the stage. The audience gave her a five-minute standing ovation. It was so great!

Do you remember how God wooed you through the testimony of others?

God woos us through His creation, through the testimony of others, and usually, through His Word. Cindy gave me a New Testament and told me to read the Gospel of John. She said, "Kathy, read it like you're reading a story. You're not going to understand some of it and you may want to close the book. Just get past it. Read it straight through." So I took the Bible home, lay on my bedroom rug, and did exactly what she said. I read John all the way through. I was astounded at how different Jesus was from what I thought He would be. People who have been Christians for a long time forget how eye-opening and revolutionary it is to take a look at the life of Christ for the first time. Christ immediately became real, and I knew when I got to the end of John's Gospel that I would have to make a decision. Either I was going to view it as a captivating myth or I was going to follow this man who claimed to be God. I'll be forever grateful that I chose the latter. After God woos us, we have a choice to make. He proposes, but we can either accept Him or reject Him. If we hesitate, it is often because of the cost of commitment. God waits. Will we love Him? Will we choose Him?

When Will I Be Loved?

We live in a time when people are unwilling to pay the price of true love. Commitment is postponed, sometimes avoided altogether. In the 1960s, it became fashionable for couples in America to live together outside of marriage. People would say, "I don't need the paper." And yet they did need God's blessing. One woman recently said of her live-in boyfriend, "I noticed a growing contempt in him for me—and I certainly was angry at him for not committing to me. The hope of a long and happy marriage died the day I moved in."

In the same way, "spirituality" is very popular right now. It's chic. It's cool to be spiritual. You can watch the Grammys, Emmys, or Oscars and hear people thank "God" all the time. But I (Kathy) often wonder, *What god are they thanking?* You can't turn on a channel late at night without hearing the psychic network enticing naive callers. Some people rub stones, hang crystals, and light candles, believing they can possess or unleash certain powers. We are also living in a time when "angels" have become quite popular. You can't go into a gift shop or a card store without encountering a painting or a figurine of an angel. Although many of these angels may look cute, innocent, or even beautiful, most of them are a far cry from the heavenly host the Bible talks about. I could go on and on. Why is all this "spirituality" so popular—and why are people so accepting of it? I believe it is because it requires nothing from you. Sacrifice is an unpopular concept in this country.

But Jesus Christ requires your life. He requires your heart, soul, and mind. He requires the cross. As in the parable Jesus told, people have all kinds of excuses as to why they refuse the invitation to the Wedding Banquet. The truth is, they are unwilling to die to themselves. *They don't understand that dying is the key to living, that with abandonment abundant* life springs forth, that with surrender comes a supernatural peace, a supernatural hope.

Haven't Got Time for the Pain

Both Dee and I have had women come to us who are deeply concerned about what they'd have to give up if they followed Jesus. They ask questions like:

Can I still sleep with my boyfriend?

Can I still party on weekends?

What if my husband rejects me, thinking I've become a religious fanatic?

Will I have fun? Will I be happy?

Let's just address this last question right off the bat. "Happy" is not the goal. "Happy" is fleeting. "Happy" gives you thrilling roller coaster rides. The *goal* is loving Jesus. Then, and only then, do you experience an inextinguishable joy. Jesus doesn't require things of us or ask things of us because He's a big dictator who gets a kick out of being in control and making us miserable. He is Lord. He is God. The "rules" are because He knows what is best for us. As you grow and know Him more, your trust grows and you are truly able to see why He requires certain things of you. He always acts out of love. That doesn't mean you will not feel a loss, or that the process won't be painful. Sacrifice is frightening. The cross is excruciating. But as bleak and as dark and as hopeless as things may seem, as they seemed to Christ's followers when He hung in agony on the cross, remember, God has a perfect plan. Just as He brought Christ back to life three days later, He will bring life out of our death. When we take up the cross, when we identify with Christ—whether it is dying to our own agenda, bearing the reproach of being a Christian, or trusting the Lord in the painful times—God sees, God moves, and God will always, in His time, bring a resurrection.

Ruth exemplifies abandonment and the resurrection that follows. She abandoned herself to Naomi and to Naomi's God. When Ruth died to her old way of life and her old gods, when she embraced the one true God, she did not know what was around the corner. But she trusted. And, under the fashioning hand of the Lord, she became an amazingly beautiful bride. Everybody thought so. Boaz told her:

> All my fellow townsmen know that you are a woman of noble character.
> (Ruth 3:11)

Ruth didn't know what was in the future, but she walked, step by step, in the light God provided. She abandoned herself to Him. And He filled her life with sweet surprises: a godly man, the restoration of her mother-in-law, a beautiful baby boy, and a legacy of godliness.

There is never, ever a death without a resurrection.

Every time we die to ourselves we are falling back into His arms. Will He catch us? No matter how long you've known Jesus, there are days when it is still easy to ask that question. He understands our fears. But the answer will always be yes. We fall back. He catches us. He speaks to us with words of love and reminds us that there is a ring on our finger. We are His Beloved, His Betrothed. And never will there be a Bridegroom like Jesus.

Signed, Sealed, Delivered

When we put our trust in Christ, we have been through the first part of the wedding ceremony. And this is a permanent commitment; the wedding is assured. Breaking a betrothal in biblical days was akin to divorce. God says, "I will betroth you to me forever" (Hosea 2:10a). The final part of the wedding will come. The vow will be fulfilled. His Word says we have been

> signed, sealed, and delivered by the Holy Spirit. This signet from God is the
> first installment on what's coming, a reminder that we'll get everything God
> has planned for us, a praising and glorious life. (Ephesians 1:13–14 MSG)

The Wedding Song

There is enormous symbolism in the traditional wedding ceremony, symbolism that was clear to believers in times past but that many of us no longer see. The form has been retained, but the meaning has been lost. When my (Dee's) pastor, Pastor Paul, presided over the wedding of my daughter Sally and son-in-law, Jeremie, he explained a few of the customs that symbolize that great and awesome day when we will experience the ultimate ceremony, when we will be wed to Christ.

- Brides are to be beautifully dressed in white, symbolizing their anticipation and purity for their bridegroom.

- As in the parable Jesus told, maidens with lamps of oil light the candles in anticipation of the appearance of the groom.

- The trumpet is blown just before the bride comes down the aisle to be united with her groom, foreshadowing the day when a trumpet will sound and we will be caught up together with Christ in the clouds.

Sally and Jeremie based their wedding on the Song of Songs. Looking back at the wedding, I realize that the mysteries they were tapping into are much deeper than any of us realized at the time. But His Spirit led.

Here are a few highlights from that day. The "wedding festival" took place in four parts:

Part I: In the Garden

In a little white church on a hill overlooking the expansive waters of Green Bay, Sally and Jeremie entered the flower-filled stage with fifteen friends, whom they called the daughters and (taking liberty) sons of Jerusalem. Sally was wearing a blue silk summer dress, Jeremie, a gray suit. They were chattering excitedly with their friends. It was clear to their guests, from the very beginning, that this was going to be an unusual wedding.

In the Song of Songs, the daughters of Jerusalem act as a chorus, rejoicing and delighting in the love of the bride and her bridegroom. In Sally's wedding, the "sons and daughters of Jerusalem" took the place of the traditional groomsmen and bridesmaids, and they had a much more active role. They asked Sally and Jeremie questions, in unison. The first question the daughters asked of Sally was:

How is your beloved better than others? (Song of Songs 5:9a)

At this point Sally read from the Song of Songs. (As I look back at the video of this wedding, this scene makes me smile. Jeremie was comfortable, but Sally's left-brained brother, John, who is an engineer, was blushing. I know he was thinking, *Only my little sister would do this. I'm so glad it is Jeremie, and not me, who is being told, in front of hundreds of people, that his head is purest gold.*) Sally answered the daughters of Jerusalem by reciting the following passage (as you read this passage, see if you can see Jesus glimmering through):

> My lover is radiant and ruddy,
>   outstanding among ten thousand.
> His head is purest gold;
>   his hair is wavy
>   and black as a raven.
> His eyes are like doves
>   by the water streams,
> washed in milk,
>   mounted like jewels.
> His cheeks are like beds of spice
>   yielding perfume.
> His lips are like lilies
>   dripping with myrrh.
> His arms are rods of gold

> *set with chrysolite.*
> *His body is like polished ivory*
>   *decorated with sapphires.*
> *His legs are pillars of marble*
>   *set on bases of pure gold.*
> *His appearance is like Lebanon,*
>   *choice as its cedars.*
> *His mouth is sweetness itself;*
>   *he is altogether lovely.*
> *This is my lover, this is my friend,*
>   *O daughters of Jerusalem.*
> (Song of Songs 5:10–16)

Another question the sons and daughters of Jerusalem asked was:

How is your God better than the gods of this world?

Each then had an opportunity to share their testimony. Jeremie spoke of the awesome holiness and power of God. Sally talked about how wonderful Jesus is, and why He is the only One worthy of our trust. She presented the gospel. During it, she said, with tears in her eyes:

I want you to know how much Jesus loves you. That's what this wedding is all about. My Jesus is altogether lovely. Jeremie and I are just a symbol of the relationship between Christ and His Church.

At the close of Part I, Sally turned to Jeremie and said:

Jeremie, now you see me as your betrothed. But in a little while, you will see me as your bride.

At this point all departed "the garden."

Part II: The Interlude

During the interlude, Sally and Jeremie retreated to dress for their wedding. Our friend Amy Shreve, with whom I've given many seminars, played the harp and sang the lovely songs she's recorded that are based on the Song of Songs.

As I think about this portion of the wedding, I realize that this is where we are now. We are betrothed, not yet wed. We have been through the first part of the ceremony. We are now waiting for our Bridegroom to return so that we can be together with Him forever. In the interlude, in this period of separation, will we stay true? One day a cry will come:

> Behold, the bridegroom cometh. (Matthew 25:6a KJV)

Will we be ready? Will we be dressed in our pure white wedding garment? Will we hold on to the hope that we will one day hear His voice, that one day winter will be past and our Bridegroom will come for us, thundering through the sky?

Amy Shreve sang "Come Away":

> I know one day I'll hear His voice thundering through the sky
> And like a thief deep in the night
> He'll whisk me away as His bride
> Come away, My love, come away . . .

Part III: The Joining of the Beloved and Lover

In preparation for the traditional wedding, another song was sung based on the parable of the ten maidens who were waiting for the bridegroom to return. Five maidens were ready for him, and they lit their lamps. Five were not ready. As the young maidens lit the candles, Amy and her husband, Gary, sang:

> Ten maidens carried their lamps of oil
> While waiting for the bridegroom five left to buy more

The banquet only welcomed those still ready, then the door closed. . . .

Now those who can listen must understand
The kingdom of heaven is now at hand.

After the candles were lit, Jeremie and the sons and daughters of Jerusalem returned and stood at the front of the church. Then the trumpet played and Sally, holding her father's arm, walked in.

In *When Christ Comes,* Max Lucado tells how, as a minister, he spends plenty of time with the nervous groom before the ceremony, watching him tug at his collar and mop his brow. Though all eyes are on the bride when she enters, Max likes to sneak a peek at the groom:

If the light is just so and the angle just right, I can see a tiny reflection in his eyes. Her reflection. And the sight of her reminds him why he is here. His jaw relaxes and his forced smile softens. He forgets he's wearing a tux. He forgets his sweat-soaked shirt. . . . When he sees her, any thought of escape becomes a joke again. For it's written all over his face, "Who could bear to live without this bride?"[7]

Certainly Jeremie lit up upon seeing Sally. When they sealed their vows with a kiss, there was great rejoicing in that little church.

And one day we will be ushered into the physical presence of our Bridegroom. His eyes will light up, love will be written all over His face, and myriad angels will rejoice.

Part IV: The Wedding Banquet

The Lord graced Sally and Jeremie with a lovely day, and the "banquet" took place under a tent along the shores of Green Bay. There were stories, songs, and much rejoicing. At the close of the reception, the guests surrounded the gazebo, with joined hands. Circling Sally and Jeremie, with the blessing of God as tangible as the sound of the waves, as lovely as the fragrance of the wildflowers, we sang:

For the beauty of the earth,
for the glory of the skies,
for the love which from our birth
over and around us lies:
Lord of all, to Thee we raise,
this our hymn of grateful praise.

It was a joyful day, a foreshadowing of that wonderful day when the Wedding Banquet will outshine our most glorious expectations.

Jeremie and Sally then left for their honeymoon, which they say was an incredibly sweet time.

Do you remember your first sweet days with Jesus? Do you remember the excitement you felt in your heart? Do you remember that precious honeymoon time?

5

Love Me Tender

WE ALL LOOK FOR THAT ONE TRUE LOVE. KATHY OFTEN SAYS that seeing others experiencing the joy of being in love increases her yearning.

November 15, 1997

I watched the Barbra Streisand/James Brolin interview with Barbara Walters today . . . He seems like a man's man—the very phrase I've been using a lot lately . . . She was content in her singleness yet he found her and stole her heart.

The story of them "spooning" . . . him saying he didn't want to fall asleep because he would miss her. It broke my heart. How sweet, how tender, how unbelievably fulfilling and comforting it must be to share that kind of intimacy.

I Finally Found Someone

We are captivated by movies where a guy and a girl, who are perfect for each other, keep missing each other—by just a moment, just an inch! True love comes so close, but circumstances or misunderstandings continually separate the couple. *Will it ever happen?* Yes, finally . . . at the close of the movie, all obstacles are swept aside and the two embrace and walk off into the happily ever after. Euphorically, we watch. We leave the theater with hope in our hearts.

Because true love is the desire of each of our hearts, we especially love to see it happening in real life, for it gives us hope that it can happen for us as well. My (Dee's) favorite real love romance is told in the book *A Severe Mercy*. It absolutely takes my breath away. This story of a shining young couple captured the award for *Christianity Today's* book of the year in 1977. The love of this couple was profound, and intriguing, for it involved the story of their conversion through their friendship with C. S. Lewis. It was also tragic, for Jean Davis (Davy) died very young. Van and Davy were full of beauty, charm, and grace—like Gregory Peck and Audrey Hepburn in *Roman Holiday*. And they were wonderfully romantic, sailing off together on their "house," a sailboat, which they named the *Grey Goose*. The name was significant, for the grey goose, when its mate dies, flies on alone for life. After Davy's death, Van never remarried. Several years ago I drove by the tiny house in Lynchburg where Van lived as a widower before he went to be with the Lord. *Here,* I thought, *lived a man who knew true love. And now he is not only with Jesus, but also with Davy.*

Sheldon Vanauken (Van) described how he felt during his first date with Davy:

> Her eyes, I had not failed to observe, were indeed beautiful: long eyes, grey eyes with a hint of sea-green in certain lights. A wide brow and a small determined chin—a heart-shaped face. Rather suddenly, without previous reflection on the matter, it began to appear to me that heart-shaped faces were perhaps the best. . . .

We talked and looked at each other by firelight, for I had switched out the lamps. She told me about a coasting voyage she had taken all by herself, just because she wanted to be on a ship and the sea. . . . There had been a storm . . . she had crept forward into the bow and crouched in a coil of line, wet and loving the spray and the plunging bow. This story appealed to me beyond words. Then we discovered we each loved poetry, she capped one of my quotations. We grinned at each other. . . .

One who has never been in love might mistake either infatuation or a mixture of affection and sexual attraction for being in love. But when the "real thing" happens, there is no doubt. . . . So with Davy and me. A sudden glory.[1]

In the same way, when you are persuaded—through the prophecies or the miracles or the changed lives of others—that Jesus is, indeed, who He claimed to be, when you come into a personal relationship with Him, when His Spirit bears witness with your spirit, you are overwhelmed by the "sudden glory." All religious leaders from the beginning of time suddenly pale in comparison to Jesus. Confucius, Buddha, Mohammed—they were just men. Gifted men, but now, dead men. They were not God. No one can compare to Jesus. Why?

Jesus alone is God. Jesus alone lives. Jesus alone could truthfully say:

Whoever drinks the water I give him will never thirst. Indeed, the water I give him will become in him a spring of water welling up to eternal life. (John 4:14)

I am the resurrection and the life. He who believes in me will live, even though he dies; and whoever lives and believes in me will never die. (John 11:25)

I am the way and the truth and the life. No one comes to the Father except through me. (John 14:6)

I am the vine; you are the branches. If a man remains in me and I in him, he will bear much fruit; apart from me you can do nothing. (John 15:5)

Jesus is the One for whom we were made. We were created to be loved by Him. And we were created to love Him with all of our heart, with all of our mind, and with all of our soul.

I Feel the Earth Move

This is how Van described falling in love with Davy:

> There was in both of us a kind of hesitant, incredulous wonder. Could this really be happening—this marvel?
>
> . . . The actual thing—inloveness—requires something like a spark leaping back and forth from one to the other becoming more intense every moment, love building up like voltage in a coil.[2]

Likewise, when you are in your first-love time with Jesus, there is an "incredulous wonder" and a spark leaps back and forth. Even though I still had laundry, dishes, and a fussy baby, my (Dee's) life during that first-love time was so interesting. I was serving Him. I had a sense that He might intervene and quiet my baby, or speak to me through His Spirit or His Word, or surprise me with some divinely orchestrated circumstance. My heart was so full. I couldn't believe my perspective was so different. I wanted to stop people in the grocery store, to stand up on the city bus, and say to all those weary faces: "Don't you know? Jesus is real! He has changed my life—and He can change yours!"

Just as I had listened carefully to Steve during our first dates, looking for signs of his love, fascinated by his mind, I listened intently again. Only now, I was actually listening to the One who made the universe, and He cared about me and had wisdom for my individual life. Before, the Bible had seemed boring and hard to understand. Now, it was the living Word of God!

Recently I (Kathy) looked at the big thick Bible I had in the late seventies. It made me laugh to see how I had highlighted it. Ephesians and Romans are just one blob of yellow. I chuckled and thought, *All of it was such a revelation. I highlighted it all.*

We were experiencing the ecstasy of kisses from the King.

Kisses Sweeter than Wine

A kiss on the mouth is very intimate. I (Dee!) will never forget Steve's first kiss. I had wondered when he would kiss me for the first time. I remember exactly where we were, the trench coat he was wearing, and how he looked at me as he lifted my chin gently with his hand and leaned down.

Someone asked me (Kathy) why I don't allow myself to kiss just for fun. I think a kiss on the mouth is such an intimate exchange. Do I love to kiss? Yes! But I've realized, more and more, that to kiss just to kiss becomes a cheap act. I don't want to let my pursuit of holiness fly out the window just to experience an exciting moment with someone I hardly even know. I don't want to ever settle for less in my life when I've learned that God Almighty always has a higher plan. When I wait on Him, He will always deliver more than I could ever grab for myself.

The first kiss is the moment when the prince awakens the princess. She has been in a deep sleep. But now she is alive, and she is experiencing the wonder of the prince.

We long to be kissed by our one true love. The Shulammite maiden says:

> *Let him kiss me with the kisses of his mouth—*
> *for your love is more delightful than wine.* (Song of Songs 1:2)

What is a kiss from the King? What is a kiss from Jesus?

We showed an article entitled "Kisses from the King" to one of the men at our publishing house. The article was illustrated with a picture of a king sweeping the maiden into his strong arms and kissing her on the mouth.

He looked at it, smiled, and said, "I'll take a hug."

We roared.

Obviously this concept is one that is easier for women, but perhaps if we considered what it *really* meant to be kissed by the King, we'd all be more comfortable with it. When Scripture is metaphorical, we need to be as well.

"Kiss Me"

Three clear ways Jesus "kisses" us are through

1. His prophecies
2. His provisions
3. His presence

How does Jesus kiss us through His prophecies, through His Word?

Thy Word (His Prophecies)

Jamie Lash and her husband are the directors of a Messianic Jewish ministry that includes the national television program *Jewish Jewels*. Jamie spent two hours a day, for five years, meditating on the Song of Songs. In her book *A Kiss a Day*, she explains that according to rabbinic tradition, a kiss from God is a living word of prophecy.[3] Have you ever had the experience of a verse from the Bible jumping off the page at you, and knowing that it was a Word from God to you? If so, you've been kissed by the King.

In traditional Judaism, Jamie explains, the first five books of the Torah are kissed by the worshippers.[4] (Actually, one kisses one's fingers and then touches the mantle of the Torah.) Kissing is an act of devotion, showing how dear the Word of God is.

One of the books I (Dee) leaned on, as a young wife and mother, is the Book of Proverbs. I was woefully lacking as a wife and a mother. Verses about horrible wives began to convict me:

It is better to dwell in the wilderness, than with a contentious and an angry woman. (Proverbs 21:19 KJV)

I had been so selfish, so concentrated on my own needs, that I had failed to see Steve's needs. Another proverb jumped out at me:

The wise woman builds her house,
but with her own hands the foolish one tears hers down. (Proverbs 14:1)

All this wisdom awakened me, like a kiss to a sleeping princess. As I began to allow Jesus to guide me and to help me be the kind of wife that was pleasing to Him, the atmosphere in our home began to change dramatically. My poor husband was so thankful and appreciative. The romance in our marriage was rekindled. This was powerful—and I was hungry for more of God's Word. I remember thinking, *I am going to master the Book of Proverbs this month!* How ridiculous. (That would be like climbing Mount Everest during your coffee break.) But I was so eager, each morning, to hear from my King. My Book of Proverbs, like Kathy's Book of Romans, soon became one great blob of yellow.

We were being kissed by His prophecies, by His Living Word.

Jehovah, Jireh (His Provisions)

Another way to be "kissed by the King" is through His provisions.

After my (Kathy's) struggles with bulimia and during my mother's illness, I took a break from singing. I had no money. When I first got back into the music business, I was working really hard, yet receiving little income. My parents were gone, I didn't have a husband, and I started to think, *Who's going to take care of me?*

Shortly after that I did a concert in Phoenix. A couple whom I had briefly met a few years earlier came up to me before I went on stage. The husband said, "Kathy, we've prayed about this and we really believe God wants to bless you. We want to give you fifty thousand dollars."

I thought, *What? Did I hear him right?* So I asked, "What do you mean?"

He repeated, "We want to give you fifty thousand dollars."

I said, "Well, as a loan . . . when do I have to pay you back?"

He said, "No, Kathy. It's a gift. Our only requirement is that you keep on sharing the gospel the way you do."

Needless to say, I was completely overwhelmed. A tender kiss from the King.

Jesus provides for us not only materially, but spiritually. I (Dee) look back to those early years and marvel at how He set us in the midst of a warm and loving little body of believers. My sister called a downtown Bible-preaching church and asked the pastor to visit us. He did, and then he directed us to a good church right in our neighborhood. This small church was filled with believers who surrounded Steve and me like a flock of mother hens. One of the women came over and offered to make me maternity dresses for free. Another couple invited us for dinner and loaded us down with books like *The Taste of New Wine* and a schedule for the local Christian radio station. The men invited Steve to help with a downtown mission to the homeless. (Steve sat in a run-down storefront room handing out blankets, coffee, medicine, and tracts that explained the gospel message. On a cold January night, huddled by a space heater, Steve read those tracts, was awakened to the fear of God, and gave his life to Christ.)

All these provisions, material and spiritual, were "kisses" from the King.

Wind beneath My Wings (His Presence)

I (Dee) definitely had the sense that I was not alone anymore. I found myself talking to Jesus, singing to Him. Our little boys soon were singing too: "Oh, how I love Jesus. Oh, how I love Jesus. . . ." There was a melody in our hearts, for He was so near. I had a sense of belonging to Someone.

There were amazing times when I felt He was physically beside me. I remember skidding in the snow on the Interstate in Portland, my small boys buckled in the backseat, my car turning completely around and facing the oncoming cars and trucks. A calm came over me when I truly sensed another Presence in the car. For a moment the sea of traffic parted, and my car turned easily back around. He spared us and others. We had been kissed by His presence.

And I (Kathy), as a single woman, didn't feel as alone anymore. One of my favorite verses, because it's so intimate, so caressing, and so enveloping of me as a woman, is

His left arm is under my head,
and his right arm embraces me. (Song of Songs 2:6)

Even as a young believer, I went to a church that shared communion each Sunday. (I happen to be a fan of sharing communion every week.) Every time communion was passed, I sobbed. It was to the point where people would come over to me, put their arms around my shoulders, and try to bring me comfort. I knew they were wondering if something was wrong. Nothing was wrong. In fact, everything was right. I had been awakened to who Jesus was and what He had done for me. I had been invited into His presence, though I was so undeserving. I realized He truly loved me. It would simply break my heart each time I thought about it. For a number of months my tears became part of the service. People just expected it. They began to understand that I was over-whelmed by my newfound Love. When new people would come towards me to offer comfort, they would get stopped by the regulars, who would whisper, "She's okay. That's just Kath. She cries during communion."

I also began writing furiously. I barely played piano or guitar, but I would just sit and write songs about Jesus. A couple of months later the youth pastor from my church said, "What you're writing is what people are singing on the radio. It's called contemporary Christian music."

"Really!" I said. I had no idea. I always thought gospel music was Mahalia Jackson stuff. But it just kept flowing out of me because I could not stop expressing my heart to God or about God.

The first-love time is incredibly sweet. When Anna, the young widow in *The King and I,* sings "Hello, Young Lovers," she remembers poignantly the preciousness of being in love for the first time. She remembers what it felt like to have wings on her heels, for her heart to beat faster when her lover came into view.

Perhaps that's how Mary of Bethany felt each time Jesus appeared at her door.

I Only Have Eyes for You

The first time we meet Mary of Bethany is in a passage that is so familiar to women that we tend to skim over it, assuming we know what it says. Often, we are so focused on Martha that we miss Mary. Read the opening to this familiar passage, but this time concentrate on Mary:

> As they continued their travel, Jesus entered a village. A woman by the name of Martha welcomed him and made him feel quite at home. She had a sister, Mary, who sat before the Master, hanging on every word he said. But Martha was pulled away by all she had to do in the kitchen. (Luke 10:38–39 MSG)

Through His words, Mary was being kissed by the King. She was "hanging on every word he said." That's how it is when you first fall in love. You don't want to miss a word, a tender inflection, a warm look, a gentle kiss. All are precious. Mary could not imagine leaving His side.

Martha, however, reacted differently.

All Shook Up

She was the Martha Stewart of biblical days. Can't you just see Martha stenciling the disciples' lunch bags with daisies, fussing over fresh fish crepes with lemon sauce, carving soap into heart shapes, and placing bayberry candles in the window? And when the Master came, the same kind of crazy hormones that fall upon us as women in December fell upon Martha. All stops were unleashed. The house had to be at its best; the meal had to be a gourmet experience—nothing was too good for Jesus. Walter Wangerin, in *The Book of God,* imagines Martha that memorable day:

> Martha bustled into the house, her arms full, her cheeks jiggling with haste and work and pleasure. "I told Lazarus that the master was here," she announced. "He'll be coming over for cakes. So much, so much to do!"[5]

The familiar account of Mary and Martha is often misinterpreted. Jesus was not disparaging the practice of hospitality, for God affirms it. He tells us plainly: "Practice hospitality" (Romans 12:13*b*). It is the spirit of Christ to open our hearts and homes to one another, especially to those in need, and to find practical ways to show love. We believe that Jesus was blessed by Martha's gift of hospitality and that the One who had no place to lay His head found something of a respite in Martha's warm and caring home. Quite seriously, we can imagine her tenderly washing her Master's weary feet, serving Him warm fig cakes, and making sure His bed linens were sweet smelling and fresh. We can learn from Martha about making others feel cherished through hospitality.

Neither was Jesus disparaging a servant heart, for He loves a servant heart. After all, the Lord Himself took on the form of a servant, and we are to follow in His steps. Martha was continually willing to humble herself and perform simple chores that would minister to others. She wasn't seeking the limelight, nor was she lazy. She was a servant. The last time we see her, even as Mary worshipped openly at the feet of Jesus, breaking the alabaster jar, we are told,

> *Six days before the Passover, Jesus arrived at Bethany, where Lazarus lived, whom Jesus had raised from the dead. Here a dinner was given in Jesus' honor. Martha served . . .* (John 12:1–2a)

We can learn from Martha about blessing others with a servant heart. Why *did* Jesus rebuke Martha? In being so worried and anxious about many things, Martha had missed the best. Instead of communing with

Jesus, she was in a whirl of activity, rushing from one task to another. Jesus gently rebuked Martha *because He loved her* and wanted the best for her. He was also protecting Mary *because He loved her* and did not want the best taken from her. How revolutionary! Surely most in that day would have thought any woman present belonged in the kitchen—not at the feet of a Rabbi!

Jesus is so loving towards Martha, repeating her name. When Jesus says a name twice, it is an evidence of tenderness. See how this is true in the following:

> *Simon, Simon, Satan has asked to sift you as wheat. But I have prayed for you, Simon, that your faith may not fail.* (Luke 22:31–32)

> *O Jerusalem, Jerusalem, you who kill the prophets and stone those sent to you, how often I have longed to gather your children together, as a hen gathers her chicks under her wings, but you were not willing.* (Matthew 23:37)

Now, read this scene in full, and concentrate on Martha:

> *As Jesus and his disciples were on their way, he came to a village where a woman named Martha opened her home to him. She had a sister called Mary, who sat at the Lord's feet listening to what he said. But Martha was distracted by all the preparations that had to be made. She came to him and asked, "Lord, don't you care that my sister has left me to do the work by myself? Tell her to help me!"*

> *"Martha, Martha," the Lord answered, "you are worried and upset about many things, but only one thing is needed. Mary has chosen what is better, and it will not be taken away from her."* (Luke 10:38–42)

Usually artists depict this scene with all of the disciples in the room along with Mary, seated around Jesus, and poor Martha alone at the door to the kitchen, cheeks flushed, her hands on her hips in anger. As women, we tend to sympathize with Martha. Fixing lunch for thirteen men who show up without notice is *not* a one-woman job.

But notice the pronouns in Luke 10:38 carefully: "As Jesus and his disciples were on their way, he came to a village where a woman named Martha opened her home to *him*" (italics added). Hmm—is it possible Jesus was alone? That's how Walter Wangerin interprets it in *The Book of God:*

> During these last three years He has usually come in the company of His disciples. He first makes sure they all have food and places to sleep in Bethany. Then He silently slips into our courtyard.[6]

If Jesus was alone, what was all the hubbub about? A five-course meal beginning with bouillabaisse, homemade biscuits, and rose-cut radishes? Charles Swindoll puts it like this: "Martha, Martha—chips and dips would be fine!"[7]

In *The Sacred Romance,* the authors claim that too often "communion with God is replaced by activity for God."[8] That is exactly what we see with Martha. Instead of communing with God, sitting at His feet and drinking in His words, she is anxiously bustling about, with nervous energy, worried about many things.

Close to You

When we are first in love, what is most important is being close to our beloved. Even though we are still faced with the pace of life and all its cares, we can experience such a sweet joy at the very thought of the One we love. We have a peace. We are content. We have been, as Charles Spurgeon writes, "delivered from the fret and fume of life, and take sweet repose upon the bosom of our Lord."[9]

I (Kathy) saw a dramatization of this when I was in Israel. The Last Supper was acted out for us, and I learned that Jesus and His disciples didn't sit at the table but reclined, resting on their elbows. I immediately pictured the apostle John leaning back on the breast of Jesus:

Jesus was troubled in spirit and testified, "I tell you the truth, one of you is going to betray me."

His disciples stared at one another, at a loss to know which of them he meant. One of them, the disciple whom Jesus loved, was reclining next to him. Simon Peter motioned to this disciple and said, "Ask him which one he means."

Leaning back against Jesus, he asked him, "Lord, who is it?" (John 13:21–25)

That was such an incredible revelation to me. John, as a man, had to feel so safe to do that. Jesus wasn't going to think he was gay. Jesus wasn't going to be repulsed. Jesus wasn't going to reject him. All that was understood before John leaned back or else he wouldn't have leaned back. There had to have been a holy exchange going on that whole time that enabled him to do it in the purest form. That's intimate. It could have been John, or it could have been a woman. It could have been me. I thought, *Jesus made them feel so safe. He was so accessible.* It wasn't just John thinking, *I love Jesus so let me lean back.* Jesus had somehow communicated, "I love you too, John. It's okay." He loves us. He wants us to feel safe with Him. He wants us to enter into sweet rest and communion with Him.

Like John, Mary of Bethany entered into that sweet rest. Notice that she never jumps up to defend herself. The deep love relationship she has with Jesus draws fire from others—first, from her sister, and later, from Judas and others who thought she had gone overboard in breaking the flask of perfume at Jesus' feet. But Mary leaves her defense to Jesus—and He defends her very well both times.

To Martha, He says:

Mary has chosen what is better, and it will not be taken away from her.
(Luke 10:42*b*)

To Judas, who initiated the rebuke against Mary, and to the rest of the disciples, who joined in, He says:

Leave her alone. . . . Why are you bothering her? She has done a beautiful thing to me. (Mark 14:6)

Both Martha and the disciples made the mistake of valuing good deeds over their love relationship with Jesus. It isn't that Jesus doesn't value good deeds. He knows that good deeds will naturally flow out of communion with Him. But communion will not necessarily flow out of good deeds. There are a host of Christians who are busy with church activity, or just plain busy. They claim to love Jesus, but their time with Him, their aloneness with Him, their time to nurture their relationship with Him, has all but disappeared. It may not seem obvious to those around them, but when this happens, a subtle and very dangerous change takes place.

I Did It My Way

Max Lucado has said that often what begins as a way to serve Jesus slowly and subtly becomes a way to serve self.[10] There's the danger. Just like Martha, I (Dee) have experienced it.

I had major surgery during the writing of this book. As I write this, I am recuperating from having my knee replaced. (Yes, I am now a partially bionic woman.) God was definitely with me. My surgeon, a precious brother in Christ, said he had never sensed the presence of the Lord so strongly in surgery. (I feel so humbled to have such a compassionate Lord and persistent prayer team, including my surgeon's wife, who prayed the whole two hours I was in surgery.)

But after three whole days in the hospital, I was feeling worried and anxious, like Martha, about "so much, so much to do!" The first morning home I rose at five. I hobbled on my crutches to our Laura Ashley guest room, collapsed on the bed, and returned to this manuscript. Still feeling woozy from the morphine pumped into my body intravenously, I looked up at the pink wallpaper and felt I was drowning in a sea of Pepto-Bismol. I laid my head back and closed my eyes, trying to get a grip.

I have to get away from this room, I thought. *I think I can make it downstairs—away from the nauseating pink and into the mercifully white family room.* It was my first attempt to go downstairs on crutches. I flung the manuscript and pen ahead of me. By the end of the stairs I had to sit down, for I was feeling faint. I'd get up in a moment, I reasoned, and recover my manuscript so that I could get to work. As I sat there, my cotton nightgown clinging to my perspiring back, I sensed the Lord saying, "Dee, Dee—you are worried about many things, but only one thing is needed."

I began to cry. I've been told that postoperative patients, like mothers who have given birth, cry easily. Yet, I believe I was weeping because I felt the tender arms of the Lord embracing me, rocking me, calming me. The same Jesus who spoke to Martha because He loved her was speaking to me, because He loved me. He wanted me to come into His rest. My "busyness" is often a way, I realize, to make myself feel like I have worth and purpose in this world. I want people to think I am valuable, important, and wise. I start out writing a book about falling in love with Jesus, and before I know it, I've ignored the very source that could give me the wisdom and revelation for this book. I end up serving myself. What has happened? I've neglected my first love.

Have I Told You Lately?

That morning I moved to the sofa and used the remote to turn on the CD player. Praise music filled the room. I heard the words of David and realized again how he truly knew, like Mary of Bethany, what was most important in life:

You are my hiding place . . .

I spent the next few hours in the presence of the Lord. The only thing I accomplished was sitting at His feet, letting Him fill me. I told Him of my love for Him. I prayed that God would make me like Mary of Bethany. She concentrated on her communion with the Lord and then she trusted Him with everything else. I also prayed that when I returned to the manuscript, He would help me remember that I was writing this for His glory.

Communing with the Lord needs to be as necessary and consistent as breathing. We must practice His presence in everything. What do you put in your heart? What do you think about? What music? What books? What about your friends? Have you sought out people who will really sharpen you? What you allow to seep deep into your soul will affect your love relationship with Jesus and your relationship with those around you.

When we neglect our love relationship with the Lord, He doesn't give up on us. Instead, He tries to get our attention. And sometimes, the only way He can do that is through pain. C. S. Lewis says, "Pain is God's megaphone."

ACT II

Wilderness Love

∾

Orchestra
adagio expressivo
(Play slowly, somberly, yet with grace)

6

Killing Me Softly

IN THE SONG OF SONGS, THE LOVER COMES, LEAPING ACROSS the mountains, and invites his beloved to go higher with him:

> *Arise, my darling,*
> > *my beautiful one, and come with me.* (Song of Songs 2:10)

But she is content. She has camped out "in the clefts of the rock, in the hiding places on the mountainside" (2:14). At this point, she refuses to go higher with him, afraid of what it might involve.

So many women are like that. They are satisfied with where they are. They've gone so far with the Lord, and then they camp out in the hiding places. They're busy with Christian service, and they don't really want to surrender some of their hidden habits to Jesus. I (Kathy) often say, "We are as sick as our secrets." We end up doing things out of brokenness instead of out of wholeness. Jesus longs for us to live differently. He longs to set us free. There was a time when I weighed thirty-five pounds more than I do today. My weight didn't balloon up overnight. It was the result of poor choices. I allowed food to be my comfort. I could have camped out there. Poor eating habits are hard to break. But I thank God that the weight finally came off. It wasn't easy— it took a lot of hard work and discipline. It still takes discipline. But I want to live in such a way that I continually let Him take me to higher places.

Maybe you have developed unwise television habits or graceless ways of communicating with your sullen teenager, or maybe you haven't truly lived or shared your faith in front of other people for years. Maybe you've gotten lazy and complacent. You are a Christian, but you have been camping out in a cleft of a rock while Jesus calls, "Take My hand and come higher." You are seemingly happy, but deep inside you are discontent. And with each call He makes, your heart grows sadder. You know you should heed His call, but you also know that change will be involved. That change can be painful.

Hannah Hurnard's *Hinds' Feet on High Places* is an allegory in which a fawn named Much-Afraid overcomes her fears and learns how to go to the high places with the Chief Shepherd. He tells her that in order to go to the High Places, she must walk herself, though he will never be far from her. She pleads with him to carry her. Gently the Chief Shepherd responds:

> Much-Afraid, I could do what you wish. I could carry you all the way up to the High Places myself, instead of leaving you to climb there. But if I did, you would never be able to develop hinds' feet, and become my companion and go where I go. If you will climb to the heights this once with the companions I have chosen for you, even though it may seem a very long and in some places a very difficult journey, I promise you that you will develop hinds' feet.[1]

Hesitantly, Much-Afraid agrees. Then the Chief Shepherd tells her he will give her two companions. When she's introduced to them, she learns that they are called Sorrow and Suffering!

Poor Much-Afraid! Her cheeks blanched and she began to tremble from head to foot.

"Why, oh why, must you make Sorrow and Suffering my companions? Couldn't you have given Joy and Peace to go with me . . . ? I never thought you would do this to me!" And she burst into tears.

. . . "Will you trust me, Much-Afraid?"[2]

Bad habits, especially those we have practiced for a lifetime, take drastic measures. Going higher *will* involve suffering. The Book of Hebrews compares our sinful ways to "broken bones." When you have a broken bone, your first visit to the doctor involves pain because he has to set the bone straight, sometimes even *rebreaking* it, so it can heal properly. If you camp out at home and say, "I'll just let nature take its course," your bone will heal improperly. You will be crippled for life. We must trust the Great Physician, even if the treatment, at first, is painful and difficult. One day we will be whole and able to climb to the high places.

You're a Hard Habit to Break

We can't let nature take its course if we want to go to higher places. I (Kathy) see our carnal habits like a river running down a mountain. Every day, it goes down the same bank, runs along the same curves, and touches the same rocks. If we want to change the course of that river, it is going to take a lot of hard work and effort. It means first carrying the stones to the water and piling them one by one on top of each other. After a while the water will begin to flow in a new way because it's been redirected. Eventually there's a brand-new riverbank and the water flows with ease on a new path. It takes time, it takes sacrifice, but it can be done and it will be worth it. I can't accept when people say, "That's just the way I am." In Christ, we have the power to change. We must be the way *He* is.

There have been many changes I've needed to make in my life, new paths I've needed to follow. I'm definitely still in process. I struggle. I'm thankful for the victories I've had along the way.

For me, the first step has always been getting to the point where I am intolerant of my sin. My struggle with my weight is an example. I had to make the sacrifice of not eating when I wasn't hungry. If I had a reasonable dinner, then I knew I didn't need to eat again before I went to bed. I had to let myself feel "a little hungry, a little lonely" when I turned in for the night. Jesus always gives us the grace to make right choices. We may be sad and discouraged, but His hand is always there to lead us to the foot of the cross where His blood can pour on us and we find new life.

I didn't lose weight overnight. It took time for my river to change its course. This new river is now a place of rejoicing for me.

I've kept my weight off for twelve years now. Whenever I go up five pounds, I remind myself of the pain I felt being overweight. I was always self-conscious when I walked into a room. I hardly ever wore a bathing suit. I agonized over the thought of going out to dinner for fear of the choices I'd make. I hated not being able to tuck my shirt in. It's not hard for me to remember how much pain I used to live in. It's all about choices, and I'm still faced with them every day. Do I have the desire to overeat? Absolutely! But I know what comes with that choice. And the freedom I've experienced in this particular struggle in my life is far better than having that constant ache in my soul.

Do I also have the desire to go out and make love? Yes. I'm a passionate forty-two-year-old woman. But I don't want what comes with it. *It's not worth it.* I don't want to have the prison door slamming, the lights going out, and the devastation in my heart. I've learned that nothing, absolutely nothing, is worth losing the peace of God.

We need to be alert because we truly have an enemy on the prowl. The last thing he wants is for us to go to higher places with God. He will tempt us. He will boldly lie to us. He will try to inflame our passions, encouraging us to live in the moment, and to inflame our fears, encouraging us to camp out in the hiding places. And if he can tempt us to take a step down, to the lower places, then he will have gained control. He will whisper to you. He'll tell you that that little bit of stepping down, that little time of falling back, is no big deal. It may be an hour. It may be a day. It may be a week, or even years. It doesn't come upon you like the smell of a skunk. Most of the time it's slow and steady, like carbon monoxide. It seeps into your bloodstream, and before you know it, you're asleep. That's how we become numb to God.

Camelot

In Lerner and Loewe's musical, Guenevere marries King Arthur, a good, kind, and handsome man who loves her dearly. The video version of *Camelot,* in which Vanessa Redgrave plays Guenevere, is wonderfully romantic. The bride and bridegroom walk down the aisle amidst a thousand flickering candles on a starlit night in a snowy mountain village. Likewise, their first years together are magnificent, leading, as good marriages do, to the blessing of many others. Arthur and Guenevere dream of a place where "might would be used for right," where knights would be rewarded for goodness and bravery, and where there would be a round table, so that no knight would be above any other. King Arthur makes a wonderful Christ figure for us, because he is, indeed, noble and loving.

Yet despite King Arthur's goodness, despite the fact that he is a wonderful husband, Guenevere betrays him, having an affair with Sir Lancelot. Three lives are destroyed, as well as Camelot itself.

Why? What causes us to lose our joy and walk away from paradise? Why do we betray the heart of our Beloved and walk out of Eden, destroying ourselves and those around us?

We begin to take our Lover for granted.

You Don't Bring Me Flowers

When Neil Diamond and Barbra Streisand sang "You Don't Bring Me Flowers," they expressed the sadness of being taken for granted. The flowers, the love songs, and the anticipation of being together are over. The romance is gone.

Imagine the Lord singing "You Don't Bring Me Flowers" to you. He practically said this to His followers in Ephesus. These people had a relationship with the Lord. They were working hard, they were not tolerating wicked men, and they had endured hardships for Him. But the romance was gone.

> *Yet I hold this against you: You have forsaken your first love. Remember the height from which you have fallen! Repent and do the things you did at first.* (Revelation 2:4–5)

When I (Kathy) first fell in love with Jesus, I had such a sense of anticipation for whatever He wanted to give to me. I was writing so many songs, singing praises to Him. It all came from the overflow of His love in my heart. I (Dee) was talking to the plumber and the postman, giving them copies of Campus Crusade's "Four Spiritual Laws." I know this may sound corny, but it was all so new to me, and I so wanted them to have the joy I had. I wanted them to know my Savior. I hungered for His words and continually thanked Him for rescuing me from myself. We were bringing Him flowers, singing Him love songs.

Do you remember what you were like when you first loved Jesus? Are you that way today? If not, Jesus pleads with you, as He did with the church at Ephesus in Revelation 2:4–5, to do three things:

1. Remember the height from which you've fallen
2. Repent
3. Do the things you did at first

If you don't address these things, your life will become increasingly dull, because though the godly man's life is exciting, "the backslider gets bored with himself" (Proverbs 14:14 TLB).

When you get bored and the romance is gone, you begin to look for diversions elsewhere. You are the perfect setup for the enemy.

The Lusty Month of May

In *Camelot,* after Guenevere has begun to take her wonderful husband for granted, she is bored. She goes on a picnic with her maids and sings "The Lusty Month of May." It is obvious her eyes are beginning to roam. May is the month, she sings, when tons of little wicked thoughts merrily appear. Her thought life has opened the door for temptation. She is ready, now, to make what she considers a "delightful mistake."

And of course, just then, the tempter stands at the door and shoves handsome, virile, and charming Sir Lancelot through. The lie of the enemy is that these "mistakes" will bring happiness. And they *do,* but the happiness quickly dissolves into enormous pain. Later, when Guenevere and Lancelot sing "I Loved You Once in Silence," they recall how they succumbed to expressing their passion, thinking it would give them joy. For a moment, it did. But now, they weep. There's twice as much pain, twice as much grief, twice as much despair. The consequences of sin are so much higher than the enemy ever leads us to believe. The desert is a hard place to be, and when we've gone there because of our own choices, we have trouble forgiving ourselves. Guenevere shaves her head and joins a convent in hopes of finding some forgiveness, some relief.

But if you find yourself in the desert, in the wilderness, because of your own choices, there is a better way out.

All I Ask of You

God asks us to repent. As a matter of fact, His desire for us is that we live in a state of perpetual repentance. We blow it all the time—and when we do, He wants us to stop and do a U-turn. Not only do we have to stop gossiping, we have to start speaking kindly. Not only do we have to stop reading trashy romance novels, we have to start reading edifying books. See the pattern in Ephesians 4:

Don't tell lies . . . . Tell the truth (v. 25)

Don't steal . . . . Work (v. 28)

Don't speak harshly . . . . Speak kindly (v. 29)

Don't harbor malice . . . . Forgive (v. 31)

Remorse isn't going to accomplish anything. Remorse is sadness without change. In Hosea, the Lord cried:

> *They do not cry out to me from their hearts*
> *but wail upon their beds.* (Hosea 7:14)

We don't want to do what it takes to repent. We don't want to change. We simply want to wail upon our beds.

Redeeming Love is Francine River's retelling of the Book of Hosea. The adulterous wife, representing Gomer, has run away after other lovers once again, and her husband, "Michael Hosea," comes after her. She locks herself in her bedroom, not wanting to come out to him, for she knows that will mean change:

She sat on the bed and drew up her knees tightly against her chest. Pressing her head against her knees, she rocked herself. Why did he have to come to her? She had come to accept things the way they were. She had been getting by.[3]

Gomer didn't want to give up her lovers. Guenevere didn't want to give up Sir Lancelot. Instead of repenting, they wailed upon their beds.

Your sin may or may not mean you have a Sir Lancelot in your life, but we assure you: *We all have something.*

Killing Me Softly

I (Kathy) often reflect on how God woos me, wins me, and loves me to Himself. Many, many times He works on my heart by breaking my heart. I can't seem to learn any other way. Now, when I think about having to pick up my cross (and I know I'll be picking up a cross), I pray, *Jesus, be merciful to me.*

Jesus *is* incredibly patient and gentle with us. At the same time, He is strong and pointed about the things that cause us to commit adultery. We are prone to go after other idols. God is a jealous God. He doesn't want us just to break the idols. He wants us to grind them into powder.

I recently wrote a song with this chorus:

> *It's been the rain*
> *It's been the storms*
> *It's been the days when I've been worn*
>
> *That I have found you, Lord*
> *That I have seen you, Father*
> *It's in the pain*
> *That I have grown*
> *Through all the sorrow I have known*
>
> *But if that's what it takes*
> *For you to lead me this far*
> *Go ahead and break my heart*

As Kathy gave this illustration, I (Dee) thought about the struggle I had letting go of each of my two adult sons and most recently, Sally, my first daughter to leave the nest. Many mothers tend to worship their children, loving them more than God. I've had to ask myself if that is true of me. I thought I had let Sally go, so then I wondered: *Why does the pain keep increasing? Why do our phone conversations continue to make me so sad? Why does God seem to keep taking her farther and farther away? Why isn't He making my life turn out the way I expected it to in my relationship with Sally? Is He dealing with me?* Sally and her husband moved to Kraków, Poland, after their marriage. I've had a lot of heartache and have felt much anxiety about her. My husband has said, "You think about her too much; you worry about her too much. You haven't really relinquished her to God, Dee." I remember hearing Corrie ten Boom, who lived out her faith in Nazi concentration camps, say that if we cling to someone or something too tightly, our loving Father will pry our fingers away. In fact, I've told thousands of women that this is our weakness as women: We're so relational. We hold our friends, our husbands, and our children too tightly. And so now I wrestle with these questions: *Will I trust God with Sally? Even if, in the future, He allows my beloved child to suffer, will I trust that He is good and that He is God? Will I stop trying to control her life, stop trying to shield her from pain? Will I let go, and if she falls, will I trust His arms will catch her?* In my heart I say yes. Yet it is a continual relinquishment. I must continually lift her up to God and pray: "Help me to trust You. Help me to let go. And Jesus, please kill me softly. Please be gentle with me."

The first time the lover asks the Shulammite to come higher, she refuses. He is tender with her, leaving her briefly, but then he comes to her in her hiding place at her mother's house and lets her cling to him. The next time he asks her to go to the higher places, she refuses again. This time, however, he is gone much longer, and she experiences much more pain. She then, in this wilderness time, decides she is willing to die to herself. She says to her lover:

I will go to the mountain of myrrh. (Song of Songs 4:6*b*)

What is "the mountain of myrrh"? Myrrh was used to anoint bodies. It symbolizes death to self. When the beloved goes to the mountain of myrrh, when she renounces her old life and yields completely to her lover, he responds:

> *All beautiful you are, my darling;*
> *there is no flaw in you.* (Song of Songs 4:7)

And that is how Jesus will respond to us when we die to ourselves and yield completely to Him. But if we hold on to our idols, whatever they are, God will find a way to pry our fingers away. When Moses came down from the mountain and saw the golden calf, he acted decisively:

> *When Moses approached the camp and saw the calf and the dancing, his anger burned and he threw the tablets out of his hands, breaking them to pieces at the foot of the mountain. And he took the calf they had made and burned it in the fire; then he ground it to powder, scattered it on the water and made the Israelites drink it.* (Exodus 32:19–20)

When God asks me (Kathy) to give something up, I'll put it in the closet or under the bed. The Lord says, "No." Then I'll throw it in my wastebasket. The Lord says, "No." Then I'll take it out to the street for the recycling pickup. The Lord says, "Absolutely not." Until I take my hammer and crush that idol into powder, it is still a temptation. The Lord's desire is for us to worship Him and Him alone.

When God took the Israelites through the wilderness, He was trying to teach them to let go of their idols. For years He was gentle with them, but then He increased their pain, until finally, He had to take their earthly lives from them, for we are told:

> *God was not pleased with most of them; their bodies were scattered over the desert. Now these things occurred as examples to keep us from setting our hearts on evil things as they did.* (1 Corinthians 10:5–6)

Jacob's life provides another vivid example of God using pain to turn our hearts to Him. Jacob tried to hold on to his idols of wealth and power. But God was on a quest for Jacob's complete love. The Lord began gently and increased the pain in proportion to Jacob's resistance.

Following my (Dee's) knee surgery, I needed physical therapy. My therapist was a young man named Jacob. When I met him, I said, "Jacob. Now there's a strong biblical name."

Jacob lit up, enjoying the attention.

I continued, teasing him: "Jacob was a cheat and a liar, you know."

He smiled sheepishly. "Didn't he turn out okay in the end?"

I laughed. "You are absolutely right!"

Jacob grinned.

"But," I continued, ominously, "Jacob resisted giving God control of his life for one hundred years. He had a miserable life, and so did his whole family."

"Really," Jacob said, thoughtfully.

Since I had this young Jacob's attention, I continued. "Jacob tried to use God for his own agenda. God gave him everything, loved him, and promised to be with him, yet Jacob wanted to keep his hands on the reins of his life. Be sure you don't make that mistake, Jacob—or you will miss the wonderful life God has planned for you."

If we are honest, we will all admit that we are like Jacob. We have not appreciated the love of God, we have taken Him for granted, and we may even have tried to use Him for our own selfish purposes. Jacob's name means "he shall grab by the heel." Evangelist Luis Palau says that since Jacob spent his life climbing the ladder of success, that should be fair warning to "Watch out above! Watch out below!"[4]

It began, amazingly, in the womb. "In the womb," Hosea tells us, "Jacob grasped his brother's heel." Jacob spent his youth trying to get what rightfully belonged to Esau, "the blessing of the firstborn." Jacob was a cheat and a liar, but God loved Jacob and wanted to take him to the higher places and make him holy. He was going to break Jacob's heart to get his attention.

You Always Hurt the One You Love

Have you ever noticed how God allowed Jacob to be hurt exactly the way he hurt others? In the movie *Ever After*, a modern version of *Cinderella*, the ending has a twist. Cinderella, played by Drew Barrymore, is asked what punishment should be given to her wicked stepmother, played by Angelica Huston. She doesn't send her to prison, but in a kind way, says, "All I want is for her to be treated as she treated me." We often cannot learn our lesson until we experience the pain we have inflicted on others. This is exactly what God allows to happen to Jacob.

The betrayal that sent Jacob fleeing from his angry brother, Esau, happened like this:

> With a little help from Mom, Jacob dresses up like his brother, deceives his blind father, and steals the birthright belonging to Esau.

Later, Jacob falls in love with beautiful Rachel and works seven years for her.

> With a little help from Dad, homely older sister Leah dresses up like her sister, deceives bridegroom Jacob, and steals the husband rightfully belonging to Rachel.

Isn't that amazing? When we choose to go our own way, when we choose to hold on to our idols, whatever they may be, do we really realize with Whom we are fighting?

He loves us, and like any good parent, He wants to teach us to choose what is right. His main purpose for us is not to make us wealthy nor to make us healthy, though it pleases Him to do so, but *to rescue us from sin.* Why? Because He loves us.

I (Dee) have experienced the pain I have inflicted on others. When my husband wanted to adopt a nine-year-old girl from Thailand who was missing her left arm, I was very hesitant. A dear friend took me out to lunch one day and drew me out with penetrating questions, trying to help me understand my own mysterious, and yes, deceitful, heart.

"Dee," she asked, "do you think you are afraid because Beth is so old? Do you think that at nine it is too late to mold her?"

"Sarah," I answered, "I'm glad she is nine. I wish she were eighteen."

She laughed. "Do you think you are afraid of the handicap? Do you think you will have to help her eat, get dressed, and do so many other things?"

"I don't think so. Steve says that because she's been without her arm for most of her life she's found ways to adapt. He doesn't think I'll have to help her do anything." Then I hesitated, feeling the emotion rising in me. "Steve says she will do some things with her teeth and with her feet." I tried to hold back tears, aware that others might be watching. But the tears began to fall when I admitted: "Sarah, I really don't want her to do things with her teeth and with her feet—especially in public."

We were both quiet. God's light had penetrated the darkness in my heart and I felt ashamed.

We did adopt Beth—and I am so thankful that God forced me out of my hiding place and into the higher places. What an amazing work God has done in my heart. I am Beth's mother—not just legally, but emotionally. I love her so much, and when she hurts, I hurt. When she is happy, I feel like the sun has peeked out from behind the clouds. She is nineteen now, but shortly after we adopted her, God allowed me to be hurt the way I had hurt, because His main purpose for my life is to rescue me from sin.

I had enrolled Beth in a special community art school for gifted children. But when I took Beth to class, the teacher would not let her participate. She said, "Mrs. Brestin, I hadn't realized your daughter had a handicap. It wouldn't be fair to the other children because she would need so much help."

Beth was standing right next to me, and I was absolutely livid. I said, "You don't know my daughter. She can do anything. Why, she can even do things with her teeth and her feet."

When I said that, the art director cringed. At that point I saw myself, and how ugly my sin had been. It is so much easier to see the ugliness, the unrighteousness, and the cruelty of sin when it is in other people!

God is refining me, because He loves me. He pulls the ugly splinters of sin out of my flesh, even though it hurts, because He knows it is for the best. And then He kisses me, puts salve on my wound, and reaffirms His love for me.

It amazes me, but just as He was on a quest for Jacob's love, He is on a quest for my love.

Even when I resist Him, even when I break His heart, He keeps loving me. Because this kind of unfailing love is so rare in the world, we have trouble believing it. When we know we have done wrong, we expect Him to walk away, and instead, He continues to pursue us.

When Jacob is fleeing for his life because he has cheated his brother out of his birthright, the last thing he expects is to be loved and pursued by God.

Some Enchanted Evening

A worn-out fugitive, Jacob finally collapses in the desert. With a stone for a pillow, he falls into a deep sleep. He has a vision in which a stairway falls from the sky. Angels are ascending and descending on it, and above it stands the Lord, saying:

> I am the LORD, the God of your father Abraham and the God of Isaac. I will give you and your descendants the land on which you are lying. Your descendants will be like the dust of the earth, and you will spread out to the west and to the east, to the north and to the south. All peoples on earth will be blessed through you and your offspring. I am with you and will watch over you wherever you go, and I will bring you back to this land. I will not leave you until I have done what I have promised you. (Genesis 28:13–15)

How does Jacob respond to this amazing love? At first he is awe-struck, but just moments later he is back to his Jacob-like ways, trying to use God, trying to take advantage of His kindness. He makes a vow, saying, in effect, that *if* God will be with him, *if* God will watch over him, *if* God will give him food and clothes, and *if* He will bring him back safely to his father's home, then he will let the Lord be his God. Leslie Williams, in *Night Wrestlings,* says:

> I find the word *if* very interesting. Like the rest of us, Jacob had a lot to learn about covenant with God—that we cannot control the terms of the contract or the circumstances of our lives, and that once we claim the Lord as our God, we belong to Him and not vice-versa.[5]

What Jacob is trying to do is sign a prenuptial agreement. Instead of for better for worse, for richer for poorer, in sickness and health, Jacob will follow God for better, for richer, and for health. And if God reneges? Then Jacob does too.

Just one catch. You can't sign a prenuptial agreement with the Almighty God.

Wild Is the Wind

God's love for us is as wild as the wind. He is not satisfied, as the song says, "with one caress." He wants us to let go of other lovers and give everything to Him. If His kindness does not lead us to repentance, then He will switch tactics. When Hosea's wife, Gomer, wouldn't listen to Hosea's sweet entreaties to come home, God said:

> I will *block her path with thornbushes;*
> I will *wall her in so that she cannot find her way.* (Hosea 2:6)

> I will *expose her lewdness*
> *before the eyes of her lovers.* (Hosea 2:10)

He can see our hearts. He knows what we need. And if we do not truly love Him with our whole hearts, if we are trying to use Him, then He will find a way to help us!

With Jacob, he used an absolutely devastating woman.

Rachel. She was so gorgeous she turned Jacob to putty. He wanted Rachel very badly. God dangled her near and then gave him Leah. Homely, sad-eyed Leah.

Jacob ended up marrying both Leah and Rachel, but the polygamous marriage was disastrous. Leah and Rachel were so jealous of each other that they filled their home with strife and bickering. Leah made an idol of Jacob's love, and she *hated* Rachel for being the object of Jacob's affections. Rachel made an idol of Jacob's children, and she *hated* Leah for bearing so many of Jacob's sons. When God allowed the pain to increase in each of their lives, they held more tightly to their idols. Instead of relinquishing them, trusting and loving God, they tried to alleviate their pain by collecting more idols. When the whole family was fleeing Haran, Rachel stole her father's household gods and hid them under her skirt. In *Seduction of the Lesser Gods,* Leslie Williams writes:

> Without knowing fully what we are doing, we hide the things we secretly love and admire under our skirts, like Rachel, sitting primly and righteously on our camels, wondering why we are not whole, why we still suffer, why we feel unreconciled to the God we profess.[6]

Rachel never let go of her gods. And God allowed her to die in childbirth, giving birth to her second baby boy and weeping for the sons she had wanted so badly but would never raise.

Jacob, Leah, Rachel, and their children had a difficult life. God won Jacob's heart in the end, but it took one hundred years. No wonder Jacob said, at the end of his one hundred and thirty years of life, "My years have been few and difficult" (Genesis 47:9*b*). He had wasted most of his life and had known very few joyful moments. Yet all that time, though Jacob didn't realize it, God was with him. Moses writes:

> *And in the wasteland, a howling wilderness;*
> *He encircled [Jacob], He instructed him,*
> *He kept him as the apple of His eye.*

As an eagle stirs up its nest,

Hovers over its young,

Spreading out its wings, taking them up,

Carrying them on its wings,

So the LORD alone led him.

(Deuteronomy 32:10–12 NKJV)

Near the end of his life, Jacob finally recognized the presence of God and gave Him the reins of his life. It took an all-night wrestling match with God, but in the morning, we see a very different Jacob. He is humbled. He is contrite. He is broken. He bows down seven times to the brother he has wronged. His idol of power has been ground to powder. At that point God changes Jacob's name to Israel, which means "God rules."

God so desires our love. He'll do whatever it takes to get our attention. Most times that means we find ourselves in the wilderness.

As we look around, we need to ask God why. For the Israelites in the desert, an eleven-day journey took forty years. Why? They weren't listening! God was trying to get their attention, but it didn't happen.

The wilderness, however, isn't always a result of sin.

When Mary of Bethany's brother, Lazarus, became very ill, Jesus stayed where He was for two days. Lazarus died. A true wilderness experience. But it wasn't because of Mary of Bethany's sin, but because Jesus was going to reveal His glory. He came to her, eventually, and met her in her wilderness.

Just as God loved Mary of Bethany, He loves us. He longs to take us far beyond the wilderness. I (Dee) am so eager to share with you a vision God gave Kathy—a vision of her dancing with Jesus. It's a story you'll never forget.

7

You Can't Hurry Love

THE SUN WAS SINKING BEHIND THE BARE BRANCHES ON THE Nebraska prairie, transforming the bleak winter sky into a palette of lavenders and crimsons. Kathy and I lingered at the round oak table, steaming mugs of coffee in our hands, and talked about our favorite romantic books and movies and how they might be parables for falling in love with Jesus.

"My absolute favorite is *Beauty and the Beast*," Kathy said.

"You've said that before—but I don't get it. How does that relate to Jesus?"

"I never expected to love Jesus the way I do," she whispered, simply.

"Ohhhhh," I sighed, suddenly seeing the wonderful parallel. Swiftly, pictures began to come into my head. How at first Belle was repulsed by the beast, then drawn to him, and then, overcome with love for him. "Yes!" I nodded enthusiastically. "That's perfect, Kath. Though Jesus never repulsed me, I was certainly apathetic, then afraid, and then! I never, ever expected I would love Jesus the way I do today."

Kathy smiled, pleased. "I'm glad I'm finally getting you excited, Dee."

We laughed. The fiery Italian river had stirred up the quiet Scottish lake. "Tell me more," I urged.

"Let me dig deeply for this," she said, pensively stirring her coffee. "It's not your typical romance. There's such an unexpectedness to their love. There was a clumsiness, an awkwardness in the beast. There was a delicacy and grace in Belle. His anger closed his heart to everyone, yet she lived very openly, with a childlike expressiveness. Underneath all his gruff exterior, the beast longed to be loved, to be understood. Belle awakened that tenderness in him and he responded by loving her, protecting her, and nearly losing his life for her. The vulnerable little girl in Belle found herself feeling so safe with him. A love affair was born."

We found ourselves smiling at each other as we pondered how great it is to feel that way. Especially as women.

She's Always a Woman to Me

"A few years ago when I was Christmas shopping," Kathy reminisced, "I came upon this wonderful porcelain figure of Belle dancing with the beast. It's so funny—when I'm Christmas shopping, I always end up getting something for myself. I was wandering in one of those classy little gift shops filled with beautiful things—Swarovski crystal, one-of-a-kind dolls, music boxes—when I saw it. Belle and the beast—looking just like they did in the movie. She was tiny, wearing that beautiful golden dress. He was huge, wearing that striking electric blue jacket. Her small white hand was engulfed in his paw. She was looking up at him, enraptured, and he was looking down at her with such adoration. Even though the figurine was expensive, I had to have it. I bought it for myself and put it in my curio cabinet. There's a little light shining down from above, illuminating the pair. When I look at them I am reminded that, every day, Belle lives inside me: the girl who wants to be pursued, sought after, swept up, and rescued."

I (Dee) sighed. I became eager to watch *Beauty and the Beast* with a whole new perspective. Kathy said, "I wrote a song called 'Dancing Me through This Life.' I haven't recorded it yet. I hope to someday. I think women will love it." Softly, she began to sing:

> Sailing
> on the waves
> of your love
>
> Gently
> move me closer
> to your shore
>
> Looking down at your footprints in the sand
> Lord, I'm safe held in your tender arms
>
> I see angels sway
> on the wind
>
> I hear you
> invite me to join in
>
> Knowing that each day
> Knowing that each night
> You'll keep dancing me through this life
>
> Flying
> over clouds
> in the night
>
> Stars shine
> With your color
> Burning white
>
> You can pierce through the darkness of the sky
> Like you do into this heart of mine
>
> Heaven
> plays the music
> of your grace

Spinning
round and round
in your embrace
Knowing that each day
Knowing that each night
You'll keep dancing me through this life

Take me in your arms
Lift me high above the world
Never end this song
And forever—dance me on . . .

As Kathy sang, I closed my eyes, picturing myself in the tender arms of God, high above this world and all its sorrow—so safe. Kathy interrupted my reverie. "Have I ever told you the story about my dancing with Jesus . . . and He was wearing a tuxedo?"

My eyes blinked open. She never stops surprising me. "I think I would remember," I said, dryly.

She laughed her hearty belly laugh. "I think you would."

And then she told me the most amazing story.

I Could Have Danced All Night

I was going to this little church on Long Island. At a Sunday service during worship, I had my hands up. I was in that abandoned state of praise, that glorious state when God's presence is so near and you can almost touch the boundaries of heaven. All of a sudden, a picture came into my head. There I was with Jesus. His strong left hand was in mine and His right hand was on the small of my back. He was gently leading me in a waltz. I couldn't see His face, but He was so manly, elegant, and strong— and He was wearing a tuxedo. I stood there and gazed at us as if I were watching a movie. I couldn't help but think, *Isn't this odd?* My eyes filled with tears as I continued to sing His praises.

A week later I was at our church retreat. They had a couple of guest speakers, and on one particular night, after a time of worship, a prayer line formed. I had a sense of expectation as I waited—I was ready to hear anything God wanted to say to me. When it was my turn, I knelt down, and the speaker's prayers for me were like spring water to my parched soul. Then she said, "I'm trying to get a handle on what I'm seeing. . . . You're dancing with Jesus . . . and . . . He has a tuxedo on!" I thought, *This is unbelievable. It's the same vision I had last week.* She continued to describe what she was seeing: "You're in a gigantic ballroom and at the edge of the dance floor are principalities and powers. Jesus is parading you around every corner, saying, 'This is My trophy.'"

I stayed on my knees, weeping.

I was overwhelmed as I realized, *How amazing that God would choose to reveal Himself to me in that way, knowing that romance is so much a part of how I filter the happenings of life. Here I was thinking it was just me and my craziness—but then, to have this lady say, "Forgive me, but . . ."*

I had that whole image in my heart when I wrote "Dancing Me through This Life." I will cherish it for as long as I live.

When I (Dee) consider Kathy's vision, I realize this could be any of us who have put our trust in Him. We are His princesses. Jesus takes our hand and guides us through this earthly journey, while all around us are the forces of darkness. They may taunt us, snicker at us, and rise up in a chorus of condemnation—but all the while Almighty God looks into their faces and says, "Say what you will. She is My Beloved."

Perhaps it was not coincidental that, shortly after being given this vision, Kathy had a battle with the forces of darkness. Had she lost that battle, I am convinced Kathy would not have been used of God the way she is being used today. Satan so often prowls about, targeting young and vulnerable lambs.

Fire and Rain

My (Kathy's) beginning years in Christian music were difficult. I moved to Nashville, where I felt like a fish out of water, never realizing I'd be back in New York five years later. It was then that I started going to that little church on Long Island.

I began to work with a very successful and wealthy manager. My whole family, especially my mother, was so excited that he wanted to work with me. He was a good man, and he believed wholeheartedly in my talent. I worked with him for about a year and got very close to his family.

During that time a producer we were working with found a song that he and my manager were absolutely convinced was a hit. This was when dance music was popular. The song was called "Too Bad We're Only Dancing." When I heard the suggestive lyrics, my heart sank because I knew I couldn't sing them. Over the next year I found myself engaged in a full-scale war over this song. At first I asked if we could change the lyrics a little bit. Although the writer wasn't too happy about it, she tried to appease me. But nobody was happy with the revised lyrics. I kept thinking, *Surely we can find another song.* But as wonderful as my manager could be at that time, he was also passionately insistent, and his opinion was dominating the whole situation. By now, record executives were involved, a lot of money was involved, and I was going to get the kind of advance that I'd always dreamed of. The pressure was enormous. Everybody, except one or two friends, thought I was crazy. My mother was so upset. She said, "Kath, your manager loves you. He cares for you. And besides, this is what you've been waiting for!" It was such an emotional time for me. I was crying for days on end, writing in my journal, and wondering how to get out of it. In my gut the Holy Spirit was telling me that I couldn't sing that song. It was black and white to me. But to everyone else it was a gray issue. "What's the big deal?" they would say. But it was totally black and white for me. I kept asking God to do a miracle: "Change my manager's heart! Have another hit song come my way. Oh, Lord, I know You can do a parting-of-the-Red-Sea kind of thing."

And yet I kept on hearing that voice. "Yes, Kathy, I can. But I want you to speak up for what you know is My heart's desire and the right thing to do." It wasn't what I wanted to hear, but I knew that before the Red Sea would part, I had to step into the water.

One of my close friends suggested I go and spend a few days at a retreat center that was just a few hours away. While I was there, I was introduced to a Slovakian priest named Father George Torak. What a gentle, humble soul he was. He had been imprisoned for his faith years earlier. I admired him very much, for he knew about the forces of darkness, about suffering for Jesus, and about having to make a choice for Him. I am in no way comparing my situation to his, but what a light he was in my darkness. God knew I needed to encounter a man with this kind of conviction. A few days into my fast, I heard a knock at the door. It was Father George. He was so concerned about me and had been praying for me. I invited him in and began to tell him the whole story. Tears came to his eyes as he saw how distraught I was.

I held my head in my hands and said, "I know I have to make a phone call. I have to do this. I know I do. I can't believe all of this turmoil is around one song—but it is. How can I tell my manager that I won't sing it? I know all hell will break loose."

The priest looked at me with such tenderness. Then he patted my hand and said, in his thick Slovakian accent, "With Christ, Kathy, you can do it." He paused. "Do you have anything in your house that you treasure that reminds you of Jesus?"

I didn't quite understand what he was getting at. But in an instant I thought of a picture I had in my bedroom. It had become such a source of comfort to me every time I looked at it. In the picture, Jesus is holding a lamb close to His face and the lamb's face is kind of squished. It's funny—sometimes people would say to me, "Really, you like that?"

Interrupting my thoughts, Father George said, "That's perfect, Kathy. I want you to have that close to you as you make the phone call." Then, much to my surprise, that dear priest practiced with me, over and over again, pretending to take the role of my manager. He said, "Keep your eyes on Jesus. You are that little lamb, and He is holding you. Remember who you are, Kathy. Okay, let's try it."

I was trembling, even though it was just make-believe. I realized how much fear I had, and I felt ashamed at how I had allowed myself to become so controlled. Then I pretended to talk into the phone, beginning with, "You know how I've struggled with this song over the last year, and I don't want to hurt you, but I can't do this song."

Then Father George pretended to rant and rave on the other end, saying mock expletives. He said, "I can't believe you are doing this to me, Kathy, after all I've done for you, after the way I've cared for you . . ."

I started to cry, and I said, "I *know* you've cared for me, I *know* . . ."

"No, no, *no*, Kathy!" Father George interrupted me. Then, gently, he said, "Just repeat, 'I cannot do the song.'"

And so I said, "I cannot do the song."

And then he ranted and raved again, and I started to apologize again. Firmly he repeated, "No, no, no, Kathy! All you say is, 'I cannot do the song.'" I began to realize that he didn't want me to get caught in the web of manipulation and guilt.

Finally, with a sigh of resignation, I said, "I cannot do the song."

The wise priest smiled. "Now you are ready, Kathy."

The day came when I made the real phone call. And it happened as Father George had predicted. When my manager realized I was standing firm and I was not going to be moved, his anger grew so hot that his words became like fiery darts attacking my soul. Finally, he said, "You'll never, ever hear from me again."

I haven't. It still breaks my heart.

Everybody was so upset with me. I remember going to a friend's house in a kind of a daze. I felt so weary. I knew I needed a safe place where I could remain quiet and catch my breath until the thick black cloud of smoke blew over.

Although it was extremely painful for me, it was one of those times in my life when I was convinced I had done what was pleasing to the Lord. The minute I did what God asked, a weight lifted from me. That didn't mean I wouldn't have consequences to face. Sometimes, when we do what is right, God snatches us out of the wilderness immediately. But more often than not, it takes time. He gives us strength and courage in the battle. He gives us grace and mercy in the suffering. It is true. And the night is darkest just before the dawn.

Raindrops Keep Falling on My Head

I was gossiped about. I was slandered. I had to claim bankruptcy to get out of my contract. My mother, who was a widow and wasn't making a lot of money, tried her best to help me out financially. I felt badly about the loss of relationship with my manager—not just because of what it meant for my career, but also because I truly cared about him and his family. I still pray about that relationship to this day. I started singing at weddings and funerals for forty dollars a pop. Often people would come up to me and say, "Honey, did you ever think about doing this professionally?" It was so humbling for me because I had traveled the country and made records, and here I was standing in a balcony somewhere singing "Sunrise, Sunset."

I think the pivotal question of the Book of Job is "Will you trust God even when there is no immediate reward?" If He does take us out of the wilderness immediately, when does our faith have a chance to grow? It's in the wilderness that we learn to surrender, where we learn to really say, "My life is in Your hands. My heart is in Your keeping."

I think that's what happened to Mary and Martha of Bethany. I believe it was in the desperate hours that their faith really grew. They expected Jesus to come running when Lazarus became ill. They sent Him a message: "Lord, the one you love is sick" (John 11:3b).

But Jesus didn't come running. He stayed where He was. And Lazarus died.

How abandoned they must have felt.

Send in the Clowns

This little family in Bethany was one of the few healthy families in Scripture. The three siblings were a beautiful family unit. Though there were times of tension, their love for one another was strong and deep. They also had a dear friend in Jesus, who became a source of strength for them. They'd heard about His miracles, perhaps had even witnessed them firsthand, and they had listened carefully to His words. They trusted Him implicitly, and they were confident of His heart for them.

Therefore, when Lazarus became ill, the sisters huddled together. What should they do? They knew it might be dangerous for Jesus to come to Bethany, because when He was in nearby Jerusalem, a short time ago, the Jews tried to stone Him. Yet, still, they *knew* He would come. After all, He loved them. And they had cared for Him so often. There had been times when Martha fixed a whole banquet for Him and all of His disciples, providing an incredible feast of meats, breads, and sweets that lit up their eyes and satisfied their appetites. And when Jesus came alone, Martha had always eagerly washed His feet and prepared a special meal, just for Him. She had served Him—now, surely, in her hour of need, He would serve her. And so, the sisters whispered together and agreed. They would send word:

> Lord, the one you love is sick. (John 11:3b)

What was Jesus' response to the messenger? It was good news, the news they expected, news that cheered their anxious hearts.

> This sickness will not end in death. No, it is for God's glory so that God's Son may be glorified through it. (John 11:4)

So though Lazarus was very ill, they knew he would not die. As they sponged their dear brother's feverish brow, they reassured him with Jesus' words. "This sickness will not end in death." The Master will come. He will touch you, speak a word—and your fever will disappear, your pain will be gone. "Hang on, dear Lazarus," they must have said. "We will laugh and eat together again." Lazarus managed a weak smile.

However, Jesus didn't come immediately. The following two verses, juxtaposed, seem like a contradiction:

Jesus loved Martha and her sister and Lazarus. Yet when he heard that Lazarus was sick, he stayed where he was two more days. (John 11:5–6)

The clouds slowly roll in. The storm is imminent. Where is He? Can't you picture the sisters continually glancing out the window, expecting to see Jesus striding purposefully up the path? Martha is trying all kinds of medicinal herbs, spooning broth into her brother's mouth. All the while anger must have been growing in her heart. *Jesus! All You would have to do is speak the word—and Lazarus would be well. Why are You taking so long? You know that with every hour that passes by his body grows weaker and his spirit even more. Don't You care?*

And can't you picture Mary consoling Lazarus, saying, "The Master will come any moment, Lazarus. He told the messenger that your sickness would not end in death. Remember His kind heart, my brother. Though He may tarry, He will come! I know He will."

But where is Jesus?

Lazarus dies, and quickly his body grows cold. How devastated the sisters were. How could Jesus let this happen? Is this love? How could He let them down like this? Because they were a prominent family, many, many Jews came to mourn with them, but some of their visitors wondered:

Could not he who opened the eyes of the blind man have kept this man from dying? (John 11:37)

When Jesus finally does come, after Lazarus has been dead for four days, each sister says exactly the same thing to Jesus: "Lord, if you had been here, my brother would not have died." They'd expected Him to deliver them. And He hadn't.

Charles Spurgeon says:

He does not say: "I regret that I have tarried so long." He does not say, "I ought to have hastened, but even now it is not too late." Hear and marvel!

Wonder of wonders, he says, "I am glad that I was not there!" Glad! . . . Martha and Mary are weeping their eyes out for sorrow, and yet their friend Jesus is glad![1]

Is this love? Like highflying trapeze artists, Martha and Mary reached for the hand they absolutely expected to be there, the hand that should have rescued them. But to their amazement, to their horror, He was not there.

How Would I Know?

On my (Kathy's) album *Love and Mercy,* I sing a song by Jackie Gouche-Ferris called "How Would I Know?" It expresses the confusion that probably every believer has felt in the wilderness, especially when the wilderness is not a result of personal sin.

Why would a God so kind and loving allow me to go through all this pain?

The chorus so beautifully says:

> How would I know You could deliver?
> How would I know You could set free?
> If there had never been a battle
> How would I know the victory?
> How would I know You could be faithful
> to meet all of my needs?
> Lord, I appreciate the hard times
> otherwise how would I know?

God allows us to be in the wilderness—in fact, sometimes He is glad to put us in the wilderness—so that our faith will grow. We're so fickle. Often, we don't hang on to Him when everything is bright and prosperous. After I said no to the song "Too Bad We're Only Dancing," I went through one of the hardest times of my life. But I believe Jesus was pleased, for I learned to meet Him with more abandon. I had nothing to go on but His Word. All I knew was that God was somehow going to continue to guide me and provide the grace I needed during this time. I didn't know what I was going to encounter around the corner, but I knew Who was going with me.

Yes, it was in the wilderness that I experienced all sorts of tumultuous emotions. But I also came to know His comfort, His faithfulness, and His love in a whole new way. And today, looking back, I see that choosing the easy way out may have spared me initial suffering, and even caused a false peace, but I would surely have been headed toward a slow death. Choosing the high road may take me through my deepest pain, but I will always come out where God dwells, a place of beauty, a place where life can flourish, and a place where my heart can be at peace.

During the wilderness time, Martha and Mary each experienced growth. And we can learn something from each of their encounters with Jesus. Martha, being her assertive self, is the first to run out to Jesus when He finally arrives.

What Now My Love?

Martha is confrontative. Never one to mince words, she tells Jesus exactly what she is feeling. A discussion ensues in which Jesus challenges her faith. He says:

> *I am the resurrection and the life. He who believes in me will live, even though he dies; and whoever lives and believes in me will never die. Do you believe this?* (John 11:25–26)

Though Martha is grieving, and terribly disappointed, her final response is one of the boldest responses of faith in Scripture, comparable only to Peter's. With Jesus listening to her intently, Martha responds:

> *"Yes, Lord," she told him, "I believe that you are the Christ, the Son of God, who was to come into the world."* (John 11:27)

When we feel we are in conflict with the Lord, we can learn from Martha to express our feelings to the Lord. You'll often hear Kathy say that there is never true intimacy without conflict. That's when your true heart comes out.

I (Dee) remember a pivotal time early in my marriage. Steve and I were deep in the wilderness as Steve was going through his ninety-hour-a-week internship in Seattle. I was a believer, but an immature one, and I thought: *What good does it do me to be married if my husband is never around?* I also felt that if Steve really truly loved me he would find a way to beat the system. I expressed all these feelings to Steve.

Fortunately, Steve was godly enough to listen to me. Though my husband was young in his faith, the way he responded to me showed me Jesus. Steve came to me the next day and said he couldn't see a way to change his situation as a medical intern. Before I could begin ranting and raving again, he said, "I love you and I care more about you and our marriage than my dream of being a surgeon. I am willing to give that up."

I was stunned as I thought about the sacrifice he was sincerely offering. Steve had already completed seven years of training, but I knew he was speaking the truth because he, unlike me, is truly Christlike in the way of honesty. His willingness to sacrifice for me inspired me to sacrifice for him. I wept and told him I loved him too, and that I would support him, and that we would make it through that year, and that he wouldn't hear any talk of ending our marriage ever again. Though I am not proud of my immaturity, I am still glad I expressed my feelings. Steve was able to reassure me of his love, even though the situation did not change, and I was able to better trust him.

In the same way, in our immaturity, or in our limited vision, we often cannot understand why God is allowing us to suffer. Should we bottle up our feelings? No, the Lord knows the deepest places of our hearts. We might as well express them to Him. Remember—this is like a marriage. We need to keep talking, and we need to keep listening. That's exactly what Martha did. She expressed her feelings and then she listened to Jesus carefully. He responded to her with a question. Quietly she answered Him, and it was an answer of faith. When we express our feelings and then wait, with an open and teachable heart, He will, in His time, respond—and it will be unmistakably God.

Martha's encounter teaches us to express our feelings and to wait expectantly for an answer. Mary's encounter teaches us that He cares about our suffering.

Tracks of My Tears

One of the most moving scenes in the whole Lazarus story occurs when Mary goes out to meet Jesus, after Lazarus has died. She falls at His feet, weeping. We are told that when Jesus saw her weeping, He wept as well. Did He weep because the situation was out of His control? Did He weep because He made a mistake in tarrying? No. We believe He wept because Mary and others were weeping and He loved them so. He knew they didn't understand, that they couldn't see into the future. Though He allows us to go through the wilderness so that our faith will grow, He still grieves for the pain we feel. He sees our tears and He cares. I (Kathy) love the verse that says:

> You have collected all my tears and preserved them in your bottle!
> (Psalm 56:8b TLB)

How attentive, how intimate of God to be aware of my tears. Not one of them is casually discarded by Him.

How long will we cry? How long will we be in the wilderness before the sun breaks through, before the weight is lifted? Only God knows, but in His knowing, He will surely provide all the grace we need during the times we feel so weak, lonely, and confused.

If it were us, we might have had Jesus raised up on the first day, or maybe the second. God waited until the third day because He was accomplishing His perfect will. He had a plan. He has a plan for each and every one of us. We must wait for it.

When I (Dee) read Kathy's journal entries, I see the ache she has often felt. The questioning. The wondering.

October 26, 1997

You seem like some far away dream today . . . a fairy tale that only happens for other people . . .

Been feeling hopeless and deeply saddened by my feelings or lack of them . . . It seems that I go in seasons or cycles of hope to an almost despair . . . I could sob . . .

March 20, 1998

On the road . . . Thinking about turning forty a lot lately. Wondering if you'll always be a sweet dream of mine . . .

The years are passing so fast . . .

Will I ever read this to you . . . ? Or are my writings in vain . . . ?

When God asks us to wait, how will we respond? Will we become bitter, throw our hands up, and turn away from Him? Or will we run to Him and allow Him to shelter us?

When I (Dee) was speaking at a Christmas outreach tea for women in Chicago, the church put me up at a lovely condominium on the lake. It belonged to a young widow named Darla who was away visiting family. I was told that Darla and her husband had found each other later in life and had had a very rare love. But after ten fleeting years of marriage, the Lord suddenly took him. Their home was filled with pictures of the two of them: skiing, camping, laughing, adoring one another. Though he had died two years earlier, his clothes still hung limply in the closet: tweed coats, ties, and casual cardigans. Even his razor and brush were near the sink. Books on grief were scattered about, including Sheldon Vanauken's *A Severe Mercy*. I imagined petite Darla sleeping all alone now in their massive king-sized bed. I could almost feel the hollowness in a room once so filled with life. My eyes fell on the book on the bedside table. The title intrigued me, and I had the sense that God had a message, not just for Darla, but for me. It was by Elisabeth Elliot: *The Path of Loneliness*. It was the words beneath the title that intrigued me:

It may seem a wilderness, but it can lead you to God.

I picked the book up and opened it. It was filled with yellow highlighting. One of the passages Darla had marked was:

Faith begins in the wilderness—when you are alone and afraid, when things don't make sense. . . . In the wilderness of loneliness we are terribly vulnerable. . . . But we may be missing the fact that it is here . . . here where we may learn to love Him—here where it seems He is not at work, where His will seems obscure or frightening, where He is not doing what we expected Him to do. . . . If faith does not go to work here it will not go to work at all.

God's answer is always: "trust me."[2]

As women, as members of the relational sex, we are afraid of being alone. When we are little girls, it is vital for us to have a best friend. When we are troubled or even bursting with good news, we will often run to the phone or send a quick e-mail. We also long to be married, and feel compassion for women who are not. Yet if we are always with a person, how can we grow in our relationship to the Lord?

As I have gotten to really know Kathy, and have come to understand her soul, I have wondered if God is allowing her to be single for His purposes, for His glory. Kathy has often said that she is not pining away in her singleness, not waiting with baited breath for her prince to arrive, but is finding much joy and satisfaction in letting her life revolve around the Kingdom of God. She often says that God will use you if you make yourself available to Him.

In the process of making ourselves available to Him, He will bring forth fruit—and to bring forth more fruit, He will prune us. More often than not, that will happen through difficult times in life when we wrestle with our faith, question His love, and reckon with Him.

Kathy has definitely experienced those seasons. Yet she is quick to say that though she is an orphan, God has been her Father; though she is single, God has been her ultimate Bridegroom; though she has faced financial mismanagement, God has been her Provider; though she has faced slander, God has been her Defender; and though she has faced many trials, God has been her Deliverer. Kathy's friend Allyson told me that suffering has birthed much fruit in Kathy because she has clung to God in it. "Suffering," Allyson said softly, "can either undo you or push you to God. But Kath has leaned into her suffering in a very biblical sense, a Romans 5 sense, and it has produced tremendous character."

And Kathy's friend Ellie observed,

There is no doubt in my mind that her singleness allows for a devotion and passion toward God that I have very rarely observed in a married woman, including myself. My marriage has caused Kathy to wonder about the magic and mystery surrounding an earthly bridegroom. Her singleness has caused me to reflect more often on the heavenly one.

Though Kathy has grown closer to the Lord in her singleness, and though she is content, she is also open and desirous of a husband, should the Lord move in that direction:

September 11, 1995

When I was at Prestonwood Church in Dallas, I used one of the pastor's offices as a dressing room. It was decorated in the way I love—rich colors and dark wood furniture. I sat at the desk to make a phone call and as I looked down, there was a Johnston and Murphy catalog on top of all the papers. It was filled with men's leather shoes, ties, and classy masculine accessories . . . As I paged through, I could only think of you. I imagined how you would look in them and how fun it would be to dress you . . .

As playful as that entry is, I remember what Allyson told me about Kathy's perspective:

Kath's struck a wonderful balance. She's not so needy that she feels incomplete without a spouse; she's not looking around every corner for a man. But neither is she at the other end of the pendulum: without hope, dead, and shut down. She is standing in the middle place, which says: God may never send a mate, but I sure hope He does. There's an ache and a thrill in that, and she embraces them both.

August 7, 1999

There were times in my life when I yearned for you and wanted you for certain reasons. Just the sheer expectation of my reaching a certain age—and I'd be married—have a house, have security, possibly children. I'd imagine many different scenarios of romance and tender moments. Besides—I pride myself on being so alive to give and receive in a passionate relationship. I've had to watch other people for so long—getting to share that with one another.

Time, age—maturity—the process of life—has brought me to a place of wanting you for far different reasons. Possibly even one.

I want to be holy. I want to be God's woman. If your coming into my life will give me more of that . . . more of Jesus, then I say, "Yes, Lord. Please bring him to me."

I (Dee) have often felt, as I know many people have, that being single is second best despite the advantages that singleness has to offer according to Scripture. Yet getting to know Kathy, and seeing what it has birthed in her, has caused me to reassess. Though marriage and motherhood are great, great blessings, a single woman, if she remains open to God in her singleness, can have a ministry and an intimacy with the Lord that we who are married may never know. And in the eternal scheme of things, is that not what is most important? I truly believe that if God brings you a man, a good man, you should rejoice. What a wonderful gift. But if He does not, there is also reason to rejoice. Life is not about a wife or a husband, it is about a love affair with God. In that you will always be fulfilled.

I definitely think the Lord might surprise Kathy. He might surprise you. He certainly surprised Martha of Bethany. When Jesus told Martha, "Your brother will rise again" (John 11:23), you can almost hear her sigh. And then she says, sadly, but with respectful faith:

I know he will rise again in the resurrection at the last day. (John 11:24)

Did Jesus suppress a smile? Did He think, *Oh, dear Martha—do I have a surprise for you!*

Jesus was not going to make her wait until the final resurrection. He did make the sisters wait four long days, but, even in that, there is no doubt He had a reason. I think one may be because of a belief the Jews held. They thought the soul hovered around the body for three days to make sure it was really dead. But when the body began to decay, the soul fled. After three days in the grave, the Jews knew all was over.

Their only hope now was a miracle.

I Hear a Symphony

Jesus walked over to the tomb of Lazarus and said:

> Take away the stone. (John 11:39a)

Martha was shocked. *Didn't Jesus care about her brother's dignity?* She argued:

> But, Lord, . . . by this time there is a bad odor, for he has been there four days. (John 11:39b)

Jesus turned to Martha:

> Did I not tell you that if you believed, you would see the glory of God? (John 11:40)

Did she then give a nod of her head to the men? We know they rolled the stone away. Then Jesus prayed a very interesting prayer.

> Father, I thank you that you have heard me. I knew that you always hear me, but I said this for the benefit of the people standing here, that they may believe that you sent me. (John 11:41–42)

Then, in a loud voice, Jesus called:

> Lazarus, come forth. (John 11:43 KJV)

If Jesus had not called the name of Lazarus specifically, would all of the tombs over all of the earth have given up their dead? Lazarus came out, his hands and feet wrapped with strips of linen, a cloth around his face. Perhaps Jesus was smiling when He commanded:

Take off the grave clothes and let him go. (John 11:44b)

Can you imagine the joy? The absolute and euphoric joy? Did Mary and Martha throw their arms around each other? And then around Jesus? And then, oh my goodness, around their brother?

Their Prince had absolutely, amazingly, come through.

ACT III

Invincible Love

༄

Orchestra
tranquillo risoluto
(Play peacefully but with passionate confidence)

8

Unforgettable

WHEN CINDERELLA APPEARED AT THE BALL, THE WHISPERING began: "Who is this gracious and beautiful woman?"

When Eliza Doolittle (played by Audrey Hepburn in the movie version of *My Fair Lady*) made her entrance, every head turned. "How lovely!" "How enchanting!" "She must be a princess!"

Bonnie Raitt sings "Something to Talk About." Suppose Jesus said to you, "Let's give them something to talk about!" Imagine if when you left a room full of people they'd be saying, "Isn't she interesting? Isn't she lovely? She loves God in a way I haven't seen." Wouldn't it be wonderful if people would consider the reality of Christ after being with you? When we are honest, we admit that we want people to think that we are radiant, that we are women of substance and depth. But what really matters is that we be godly women, women who possess so much of Jesus that people believe He exists because He is so powerful in us. We should leave behind the fragrance of Christ, a fragrance that stays on their mind.

Mary of Bethany certainly did that. When she left the party she attended nearly two thousand years ago, they were talking—and they haven't stopped.

I Surrender All

Mary entered the party, a room full of men, carrying her perfume in an alabaster container. She did what she absolutely had to do. It didn't matter to her how people would react. All that mattered to her was Jesus.

Costly perfume was stored in alabaster, which was a kind of marble. Mary's jar apparently had a long slender neck that could easily be broken. In their book *Lady in Waiting*, Debby Jones and Jackie Kendall write:

> In the days Jesus was on earth, when a young woman reached the age of availability for marriage, her family would purchase an alabaster box for her and fill it with precious ointment. The size of the box and the value of the ointment would parallel her family's wealth. This alabaster box would be part of her dowry. When a young man came to ask for her in marriage, she would respond by taking the alabaster box and breaking it at his feet. This gesture of anointing his feet showed him honor.[1]

Mary's perfume was very valuable indeed. It was worth approximately a year's wages. But rather than saving it for her earthly bridegroom, she chose to break the box and pour some of the perfume on the head of Jesus. Then she sank to her knees and poured the rest on His feet, wiping them with her long and flowing hair. Perhaps she used her hair, rather than a towel, as an indication of her great love for Jesus. Leon Morris writes:

> The act is all the more striking in that a Jewish lady never unbound her hair in public. That apparently was a mark of loose morals. But Mary did not stop to calculate public reaction. Her heart went out to her Lord and she gave expression to something of her feelings in this beautiful and touching act.[2]

The setting was Bethany, shortly after the raising of Lazarus and six days before the crucifixion of Christ. This incident is often confused with an incident in the Book of Luke in which a notably sinful woman, probably a prostitute who had been forgiven, anointed Jesus early in His ministry. It is very important to us that you understand that these were two different incidents and that Mary of Bethany was never a prostitute. The banquet at which Mary of Bethany anointed Jesus was a grateful celebration for the raising of Lazarus. Tradition says the host, Simon the leper, may have been healed by Jesus and was related to the siblings, possibly as their father. If this is true, you can almost imagine the outpouring of gratitude. What joy Simon would have felt at having his only son back!

Matthew, Mark, and John all record this incident, with different details, and only John specifies that the woman was Mary of Bethany. Read carefully the account given by John.

> Six days before the Passover, Jesus arrived at Bethany, where Lazarus lived, whom Jesus had raised from the dead. Here a dinner was given in Jesus' honor. Martha served, while Lazarus was among those reclining at the table with him. Then Mary took about a pint of pure nard, an expensive perfume; she poured it on Jesus' feet and wiped his feet with her hair. And the house was filled with the fragrance of the perfume.
>
> But one of his disciples, Judas Iscariot, who was later to betray him, objected, "Why wasn't this perfume sold and the money given to the poor? It was worth a year's wages." He did not say this because he cared about the poor but because he was a thief; as keeper of the money bag, he used to help himself to what was put into it.
>
> "Leave her alone," Jesus replied. "It was intended that she should save this perfume for the day of my burial. You will always have the poor among you, but you will not always have me." (John 12:1–8)

Have you ever been so overwhelmed with love for Jesus that you simply had to do something? Mary of Bethany loved Jesus so—and now

He was also her Prince who had rescued her by raising her precious brother from the dead. A. B. Bruce writes:

> She loved Jesus with her whole heart, for what He was, for what He had done for the family . . . there was such love in her heart . . . yet it could not find expression in words. She must do something to relieve her pent-up emotions: she must get her alabaster box and break it, and pour it on the person of Jesus, else her heart will break.[3]

The risk she took was astonishing. Women were supposed to stay in the background. Yet here, with one overwhelming intention, Mary of Bethany boldly enters a house full of men. It doesn't matter to her that she is risking her pride, her reputation, and her dowry—she is ready to abandon all for Jesus. What she does is dramatic, and it causes an enormous stir. The perfume's fragrance filled the whole house and lingered, no doubt, on Jesus through the following holy week, through His crucifixion, and on His body in the grave. Mary of Bethany turned that day into a day that would go down in history. Kathy has often prayed:

> Jesus,
> teach me to kneel
> at Your feet.
> to talk with You,
> watch You,
> hear You,
> worship You,
> so that
> my prayers and praise
> are like that costly ointment
> and all of heaven
> filled with the fragrance
> of our time together

Before we return to Mary, we'd like to look at another unforgettable woman: Mother Teresa. Like Mary of Bethany, Mother Teresa's focus was Jesus, not the crowd around her. In a sense, she entered a party with an alabaster bottle on February 4, 1994, at the National Prayer Breakfast in Washington, D.C. Usually this is a sedate affair in a plush hotel, a polite acknowledgment that we are a "religious country," with speakers carefully sidestepping all controversial issues. Not Mother Teresa. She didn't care about the risk she was taking, or what anyone thought. Like Mary of Bethany, she was so motivated by her love for Jesus that she did what she absolutely had to do. She began by talking about how much Jesus loved us, about how He had died for our sins. Then quietly, but pointedly, she expressed her concern about the spiritual poverty in our country:

> St. John says that you are a liar if you say you love God and you don't love your neighbor. . . . On the last day Jesus will say to those on his right, "whatever you did to the least of these, you did to me," and he will also say to those on his left, "whatever you neglected to do for the least of these, you neglected to do it for me."

She spoke of visiting a nursing home in the States and asking the nun in charge:

> "Why do these people, who have every comfort here—why are they looking toward the door? Why are they not smiling? I am so used to seeing the smiles on our people. Even the dying ones smile."

> And Sister said, "This is the way it is, nearly every day. They are expecting—they are hoping—that a son or daughter will come to visit them. They are hurt because they are forgotten."

> . . . This neglect to love brings spiritual poverty. Maybe in our family we have somebody who is feeling lonely, who is feeling sick, who is feeling

worried. Are we there? Are we willing to give until it hurts, in order to be with our families? Or do we put our own interests first?

Many began to shift in their seats. Mother Teresa continued:

> Love begins at home. . . . But often father and mother are so busy that they have no time for their children, or perhaps they are not even married, or have given up on their marriage. . . . We are talking of love of the child, which is where love and peace begin. These are the things that break peace.

Many parents stared at the carpet. But the remarks that made headlines in some cities, the remarks that caused perspiration to appear on the foreheads of many political leaders, were;

> But I feel the greatest destroyer of peace today is abortion, because it is a war against the child . . . and if we accept that a mother can kill even her own child, how can we tell other people not to kill one another? . . . Any country that accepts abortion is not teaching the people to love, but to use any violence to get what they want. That is why the greatest destroyer of love and peace is abortion.

> . . . Please don't kill the child. I want the child. Please give me the child. . . . From our children's home in Calcutta alone, we have saved over 3,000 children from abortions. These children have brought such love and joy to their adopting parents and have grown up so full of love and joy![4]

Peggy Noonan, reporting in *Time,* called Mother Teresa's speech a courageous act and described President and Mrs. Clinton and Vice President and Mrs. Gore as looking like "seated statues at Madame Tussaud's, glistening in the lights and moving not a muscle." After Mother Teresa's remarks on abortion, there was a moment of complete silence, and then "applause built and swept across the room."[5] Just as at Simon's party that day so long ago, there were definitely those who were not pleased, who did not applaud. But just as the threat of criticism didn't stop Mary of Bethany, it didn't stop Mother Teresa. She entered that room with her alabaster box and poured it on the person of Jesus.

Though Jesus is no longer with us physically, He is here—in the poor, in the lost, in the lonely, in the defenseless baby in the womb. Mother Teresa made that quite clear when she was on a morning talk show and was asked, "There are so many poor, so many suffering—you can only help a small percentage of them, so why do you bother?"

She asked the interviewer to repeat the question—this worldly thinking was so foreign to her. The question was repeated and still she was confused. But finally, she answered simply, "Jesus said, 'When you do it to the least of these, you do it to me.'" She entered the stage of life, whether it was the streets of Calcutta or the National Prayer Breakfast, carrying her alabaster box to break on the person of Jesus. She wasn't stopped by criticism or motivated by applause. She only had eyes for Jesus.

I (Kathy) was so intrigued by Mother Teresa that when I heard she was going to be at a 7:30 A.M. mass in New Jersey, I got up at 4:30 A.M. to go and see her. I knew she was getting old and I wanted a chance to encounter her in this life. Church was packed. On either side of the altar, the press was everywhere—ABC, CBS, CNN. In walked Mother Teresa, tiny, worn, and wrinkled. Oh, the glory that emanated from her soul. I was sitting three-fourths of the way back watching and thinking: *This woman who gave her life for the gospel is being praised not only by the church but by the press.* It's just as the Scripture says, "Whoever humbles himself will be exalted." Her abandoned life to Christ has given them something to talk about. Mother Teresa spread His fragrance to the world. Was it Giorgio? Givenchy? Estée Lauder? No—it was Jesus. Jesus was so evident in her, His life so undeniable in her.

God allowed me a special moment I'll never forget. The church service ended and people were leaving in droves. Because of all the paparazzi, frail Mother Teresa was whisked out a back entrance, away from the crowd. I was walking slowly back to my car when all of a sudden I saw a church van pulling away. In the backseat was Mother Teresa. I ran up to the van and spread out my hand on the window. She eagerly reached up and placed her hand on mine. That famous wide smile took hold of her face. I smiled back.

We're living in a time when laser surgery, face-lifts, breast implants, liposuctions, and tummy tucks are readily available. But the most beautiful women I've met have been those women who have surrendered so totally to Jesus that He radiates through their person. He is their beauty. The latest in hair styles, cosmetics, or skin care can never compete or compare with the loveliness of a woman who has allowed Jesus to occupy every place in her heart. How I yearn to be a woman like that. I want to give people something to talk about—and that something, that Someone, is Jesus. That's what Mary of Bethany did, and we can, too, if we trust Him and abandon ourselves to Him.

Call Me Irresponsible

Mary of Bethany surrendered her pride and her reputation. We are told the disciples rebuked her harshly, but their rebukes simply didn't matter to her. When we are concerned about our own reputation, we are self-conscious and hold in check the loving word that might be spoken, the loving deed that might be done. But those who live an abandoned life seize every opportunity to give encouragement to others, especially those who need it most.

Mary of Bethany surrendered her possessions. Whenever we sing "Take My Life," I (Dee) squirm a little at the line "Take my silver and my gold, not a mite would I withhold." Mother Teresa said, "Give until it hurts."

Mary of Bethany surrendered her time. She sat at His feet, unconcerned about the pressures of life. She knew that if she put Him first, everything else would fall into place. Often my (Dee's) most precious times with God are in the morning. It's so quiet. I can be all alone with Him. I sometimes hesitate to ask the Lord what His plans are for my day. What will He require of me? It's laughable when I put it into words because I've given Him my life—so why won't I give Him my day?

All of my Christian life I have struggled with breaking the alabaster box of my own agenda. I *know* I have missed God-appointments because I was so focused on what I was doing. Because I am busy writing Christian books, because I am traveling and speaking, it is easy to lose perspective. I can think I am about God's agenda when I may be missing it completely. Isn't that what happened to the priest and the Levite in the parable of the Good Samaritan? They stepped right over the broken and bleeding man, thinking they were serving God. I *know* I have stepped over people in need in my path. They could be seated next to me in the airplane, they could be calling me late at night, or they could be vulnerably telling me about wounds in their life, and I am too preoccupied to feel the severity of their pain. I *know* I have even stepped over the bodies of cherished friends, my own children, my own grandchildren, and my precious elderly parents. How depraved I am. How in need of God's grace. Jesus *never* saw people as interruptions. His only focus was His Father's will, His Father's agenda. He *truly*, as James tells us to do, saw interruptions as friends.

Why do I hold on to my own agenda so tightly? Because I forget that my life must be about Jesus, and not centered around me. The selfish Dee is still kicking. I pray she'll learn how to die.

And so I continually ask God to change my heart. Kathy has been such a model for me, speaking the truth to me when she sees me hesitate to be merciful.

Just this week someone called wanting to chat. Often I am reserved with her, because her chats can become lengthy. But this time I didn't shut up my compassions. His Spirit reminded me to be the love of Jesus to her. At the end of the phone call, she said, "This meant so much to me, Dee. I always feel like you are *so* busy—but I must have caught you at a good time." (I hung up and wept. And then, *yes*, I sensed *His* pleasure.)

Each time I break the alabaster box of my own agenda at His feet, the fragrance fills the room, bringing joy to weary faces, and surrounding me, enveloping me with peace and an inextinguishable joy.

In the last two years I've been praying, daily, that I would love Jesus more. More growth has occurred in the last two years than in any other period in my life. Why? It's simple, really. As His love wells up in me, it is like the sap that rises in the spring, pushing off those ugly stubborn leaves that have clung tenaciously to the branches all winter. It's exciting when I see the leaves fall, because when they do, I know I'm allowing room for new life.

> Precious Jesus,
> Help me fall
> more in love with You,
> abandoning
> my time,
> my possessions,
> my old habits,
> my reputation,
> my anxieties
> breaking each
> alabaster box
> at Your feet.

One of my (Kathy's) alabaster boxes has been the desire for success. My mother always said, "My daughter is going to be somebody." I have a picture of me in the fifth-grade choir where the mothers were obviously told to dress their kids in white shirts and dark skirts or pants. But my mother dressed me in a bright red jumper. I smile and shake my head every time I look at it. My mother was going to make sure I stood out.

When I first moved to Nashville in my twenties, my family had such high hopes and dreams for me. I was managed by the same men who managed Amy Grant, and that started the whole process of God humbling me. When I was in Long Island I was the big fish in the small pond, and now I was watching Nashville's princess walk through my dreams. I started working in a little Christian bookstore, and my family couldn't understand why things weren't happening. I did get out my first recording, *Stubborn Love,* in 1982. I'm not saying I didn't have a certain amount of success at that time, because I did. But it didn't quite happen the way I thought it was going to. All these years later, I realize that God was protecting me from having too much too soon. I realize now that God was developing a holy brokenness and humility in me that could not have happened had I not lived through that season in my life. I've often hung on to Mother Teresa's words: "Faithfulness, not success." God is sovereign. And whether or not I ever sing another note, I am God's Beloved. He desires relationship with me. That is the most important thing.

At this time in my life, God is allowing me to step into arenas where I am speaking and singing to thousands of women. My spirit often says, "Ahhhh." The years of feeling like things should be happening in a certain way (ways I had imagined), the years of feeling forgotten by God, feeling like a stepchild, have prepared me for such a time as this. He's patiently loved me and taught me and revealed Himself to me. And that is how I'm able to speak to women boldly and confidently about Jesus. Whether I'm addressing eating disorders, self-esteem, death, bitterness toward an ex-husband, an abortion, or the hundred other things women face every day of their lives, the solution is the same. The answer is the same. We must know God. We must be honest with Him. We must be willing to pick up the cross He offers us, knowing there will always be a resurrection. Always.

Do Dee and I still get frustrated? Do we still question God? Do I still have days when lifting my head from the pillow feels like an impossible chore? Absolutely. We're trapped in these bodies and we will deal with these things until we see Him face to face. Until then, we must cling desperately to the One who is crazy about us, to the One who has promised us wholeness, to the One who has promised to never let us go.

It's a choice of faith, for example, to carry an unexpected pregnancy to term, to give that baby life. The women who do that are the women who break at the feet of Jesus the alabaster boxes of time and convenience and, sometimes, the joy of raising that baby themselves. Recently, a fourteen-year-old came up to me at Bill Gaither's Praise Gathering. She was precious, just a child. She said, "I just want you to know that I was three months pregnant, and I wanted to have an abortion. My mom played 'A Baby's Prayer' for me, and I carried my baby full term and gave my baby up for adoption."

I hugged her, and we both cried. I said, "That is so commendable. You made a choice for life, and God is about life." I held her face in my hands, kissed her forehead, and reminded her of how precious she was to God. That afternoon when I was speaking, I called that young woman to come on stage with me. Everyone gave her a standing ovation.

I was so thankful for that, because sometimes we tell women not to abort but don't support them when they make the hard choice to carry that life. By finding ways to support these women, we truly become God's hands and heart for them, blessing them for the hard choice they have made.

I've also been able to encourage many postabortive women. Their grief lives deep in their hearts, their shame is written on their faces, and their guilt weighs down their souls. When these women are able to get honest and let it all go, I've seen His river of life wash over them, cleansing and healing. What a joy to see them accept God's forgiveness and forgive themselves. How exciting to see them released and set free. I know that they can go home and see their other children, not as reminders of their sin, but as precious gifts of grace.

My favorite time of year is autumn. Leaves turning, it's nature's fashion show. Armani, Calvin Klein, and Versace wish they could look this good! Yet what penetrates my heart is that amidst this lavish exhibit, there is a complete dying process going on. Every leaf that boldly expresses its splendor will eventually fall to the ground. Dry and barren. Its beauty seemingly gone forever. Until spring . . . new buds, new life, a new creation.

When we die to ourselves, when we break our alabaster box, it is an act of faith—that from death will come life. Do we believe there will be a resurrection? So often we don't believe it. We don't want to die to ourselves because we don't believe God will do His part. But He will.

He certainly did with Mary of Bethany. What she did turned out to be an enormous blessing, not just for Jesus, but for her, and for generations to come.

What I Did for Love

Did Mary know what was going to happen as a result of her sacrifice? Jesus said that Mary poured perfume on Him to prepare His body for burial. Did she know Jesus was going to be crucified? Did she intend for her perfume to anoint Him for His burial? Some are absolutely convinced she understood; others are just as convinced she did not. Read the account Mark gives:

> While he was in Bethany, reclining at the table in the home of a man known as Simon the Leper, a woman came with an alabaster jar of very expensive perfume, made of pure nard. She broke the jar and poured the perfume on his head.
>
> Some of those present were saying indignantly to one another, "Why this waste of perfume? It could have been sold for more than a year's wages and the money given to the poor." And they rebuked her harshly.
>
> "Leave her alone," said Jesus. "Why are you bothering her? She has done a beautiful thing to me. The poor you will always have with you, and you can help them any time you want. But you will not always have me. She did what she could. She poured perfume on my body beforehand to prepare for my burial. I tell you the truth, wherever the gospel is preached throughout the world, what she has done will also be told, in memory of her." (Mark 14:3–9)

Perhaps Mary was simply led of the Holy Spirit but didn't know how meaningful her act was going to be. Perhaps she knew He was going to die but didn't know how soon or that she was actually preparing His body for burial. Yet Christ turns and canonizes her on the spot, astonishing all in the room.

I (Kathy) have often been led to do something without knowing exactly why. When we choose to take the hand of Jesus even though we may not know where He's leading, He has a certain destination in mind, and it will be a delightful surprise to our souls.

Several years back when I was in a quaint little town in Austria, I saw a crucifix in the window of a little carpenter's shop. It was exquisitely hand carved: the veins, the agony, the sorrow. It was the most unbelievable cross I'd ever seen. The shop was closed, but some people on the street gestured to the apartment upstairs. I ran up the steps and knocked on the door. A tall man peeked out. Using gestures, I communicated, "Are you the carpenter who owns the shop? Will you open it up? I want the cross in the window." He politely came down, opened the doors, and sold the magnificent cross to me. I knew I would cherish it forever.

On the way home, while I was lifting the package to put it in the overhead on the plane, so excited to have found this awesome piece of art, God suddenly spoke to my spirit. *You need to give this to Breeda.* (Breeda is a dear friend of mine. She prays diligently for me and is one of the godliest women I know.)

"What?" I said. "Breeda? Really? . . . Why?"

You need to give the cross to Breeda.

"Well . . . well . . . okay, Lord. Okay."

Not too long after that, I planned to meet some friends for dinner at an Italian restaurant. Breeda was going to be there. I wrapped up the cross and found myself with a sense of joyful anticipation. When I saw her, I hugged her and said, "I know this is strange, but I have something for you. God told me to give this to you."

She opened it up and tears began to sweetly flow. "You don't know how much I've been praying that God would just show me a sign," she cried, "of how much He loves me." I started weeping too, because although I hadn't realized Breeda's need, God had. He asked me to do something, and I'm so thankful I obeyed. It turned out to be a huge blessing for both of us. I think that's how it might have been for Mary of Bethany. Sometimes we do things out of obedience and only later understand God's purpose.

I (Dee) think Mary may have understood that Jesus was going to die very soon and may even have understood that she was anointing Him for

His burial. It seems to me that Jesus implied she understood. I have often seen that those who sit at the feet of Jesus, listening to Him intently, are more apt to see things that fly completely over the heads of others.

Repeatedly in Scripture the Lord lets us know that those who earnestly desire to know Him, to see Him, and to understand Him will. He spoke in riddles and parables to hide things from those who were not welcoming Him but was eager to reveal Himself to those with seeking hearts. Do you remember how the Lord said, "Shall I hide from Abraham what I am about to do?" (Genesis 18:17)? The Lord chose not to hide the truth from Abraham, the friend of God. I think it is possible that the Lord chose also not to hide the truth from Mary of Bethany because she too was truly His friend and earnestly desired to understand and obey. Dallas Willard, in *The Divine Conspiracy*, helps us to understand why some believers are able to see spiritual mysteries and others struggle:

> Seeing is no simple thing, of course. Often a great deal of knowledge, experience, imagination, patience, and receptivity is required. . . . But seeing is all the more difficult in spiritual things, where the objects . . . must be willing to be seen.
>
> Persons rarely become present where they are not heartily wanted. Certainly that is true for you and me. We prefer to be wanted, warmly wanted, before we reveal our souls—or even come to a party.
>
> The ability to see and the practice of seeing God and God's world comes through a process of seeking and growing in intimacy with him.[6]

For some time Jesus had been telling His followers that He was going to Jerusalem to die, and they'd look at Him with glazed eyes and say, "Huh?" But I think it is at least possible that Mary of Bethany understood, because she loved Him so much and heartily wanted to understand Him. The psalmist tells us the Lord confides in those who worship Him (based on Psalm 25:14a AMP).

When I read a commentary that says, "Of course Mary didn't understand," I think, *Why do you say "of course"?* Mary had seen Jesus raise her brother from the dead. She had seen Him do the impossible. She also could see that all were not pleased. Did she hear that some were plotting to take the life of Jesus and of Lazarus? I think she may very well have seen the thunderclouds rolling in, the storm on the horizon, and was quite purposeful in what she did.

But perhaps it is simply my pride as a woman that relishes the irony that a woman, considered to be the inferior gender in that culture (but not by Jesus), gleaned what all the men had missed.

But whether Mary of Bethany understood or not, she certainly provides a sharp relief to the actions and attitudes around her: an act of love in the midst of hate, for the plotting against Jesus immediately precedes the anointing, and the betrayal immediately follows it. Likewise, Mary is a contrast to the bumbling disciples, who are quite confident that they are right to harshly rebuke her. In the midst of pride and greed she comes, humbly breaking her precious alabaster box and wiping His feet with her unbound hair.

In obeying the prompting of the Spirit, she left a legacy. In fact, as Jesus prophesied, wherever the gospel is preached throughout the world, what Mary of Bethany did is told, in memory of her. She is unforgettable.

And if we die to ourselves, we can be unforgettable too.

9

Our Love Is Here to Stay

AN "OSCAR MOMENT" OCCURRED IN 1999 WHEN LIFE IS *Beautiful (La Vita E Bella)* was announced as the winner for the best foreign film. The writer, director, and leading man, the ebullient Roberto Benigni, jumped to his feet and kissed his wife as his peers applauded thunderously. Laughing and waving his arms jubilantly, he made his way to the stage by leaping from chair to chair. His spontaneous joy won the hearts of viewers.

The message of the film is a message that weaves its way through Ecclesiastes, the prophets, and the prison epistles. What is it?

Life on earth is hard, and full of sorrow,
still, life is beautiful when you love and are loved.

Life Is Beautiful shows us a portrait of a husband and wife who have reached the height of invincible love and whose marriage, in a mysterious way, as a good marriage is supposed to do (Ephesians 5:22–33), reflects the intended relationship between Jesus and true believers. It also portrays the undying sacrificial love of a father for his only son.

As Christ woos us, Benigni wooed his wife-to-be in *Life Is Beautiful*. He called her "Principessa" (Princess) and wooed her by surprising her, by making her laugh, and by treating her like royalty. He won her heart and rescued her from marrying a brutish man, from her own selfishness, and finally from the greatest horror of the twentieth century, the holocaust against the Jews and those who tried to protect them.

The "Principessa," played by Benigni's actual wife, responded to her suitor's love, much as we respond to Christ's love.

I'd Do Anything

To the amazement of the Nazi guards, the "Principessa" insisted on stopping and boarding a train headed to the death camps. Why? Her husband and son were on it. As believers, we will make sacrifices the world will not understand, because of our love for Christ. And, as we die to ourselves and submit to Him, we will also experience a joy and a peace the world can never know.

The world is repelled by the concept of submission. When they hear, for example, that the Bible says wives are to submit to their husbands, they see red. On the basis of this sound bite, they condemn the whole of Christianity. Even many believers bristle when they hear the verse "Wives, in the same way be submissive to your husbands" (1 Peter 3:1a). One of the reasons I (Dee) was motivated to write the Bible study guide *A Woman's Journey through 1 Peter* was to help women see this verse in context. Do you know the prime model Peter gives for submission? It isn't women. It's Jesus! Peter writes:

> When they hurled their insults at him, he did not retaliate; when he suffered,
> he made no threats. Instead, he entrusted himself to him who judges justly.
> (1 Peter 2:23)

Then Peter instructs us to follow in the steps of Christ. All believers, "in the same way," are to live submissive lives, committing their case to God.

The believers listed in Peter's letter include citizens, slaves, wives, and husbands!

When I (Kathy) became a Christian, my friends said, "Are you kidding me? Do you know what the Bible says about men and women and about submission? What are you doing, Troccoli? You're going backward."

I tried to make them understand. I said, "Look, you can't just pick out one piece of Scripture and not acknowledge the words around it. That's like trying to understand the beauty of a rose garden by looking at a single thorn. It clearly tells husbands to love their wives as Christ loved the church. That is such a high calling, and it is so sacrificial. Christ gave His life for the church. I would love to experience that kind of lavishness from a man. Can't you see?" I knew they weren't willing to see. That was really my very first glimpse that if you don't know the whole of Scripture, you can twist it and turn it and use it in any way you want. But that doesn't mean it will represent the heart of God. It blows my mind to see women picketing outside Promise Keeper's rallies. They are protesting the gift God is yearning to bestow on them—the gift of a man loving Jesus with all his heart, humbling himself before God, sacrificing his own pride, making a commitment to die to himself. Why would anybody have a problem with that? That's what I love about *Life Is Beautiful*. It is the epitome of a husband imitating Jesus Christ, laying down his life for his bride.

When a Man Loves a Woman

Though Benigni is separated from his wife in the concentration camp, he finds ways to communicate with her. Once, he and their little boy dodge into the small room where the camp's loudspeaker is housed. In the mike he calls out, "Principessa!" Then their son says, "Mama, Mama!" She hears their voices and her hope soars as she realizes they are still alive. Another time, while busing tables for the Nazi guards, Benigni spies a Victrola and finds the record that they both listened to while they were falling in love. He turns the amplifying horn toward the window, facing her barracks, and the romantic melody wafts out over the grim surroundings, reminding her again of his life and his love.

Benigni also rescues their little son, a precious wide-eyed innocent, helping him survive by pretending that the concentration camp is a great game in which they accumulate points for hiding, for being brave, and for not crying for Mommy. Near the close of the movie, the war is ending. Rescue is now a real possibility, but Benigni is caught. As the Nazi guards march him to his death, his little boy watches from his hiding place. Benigni winks, smiles broadly, and lifts his legs high in a march, as if he is enjoying it. His son, convinced it is all still a great game, giggles softly and quietly stays in his hiding place until the Allies arrive. When he is reunited with his mother, he tells her what fun he and his father had—how they laughed, even in the worst of circumstances. His father's sacrifice saved his life. "This is the gift," the son writes later, "my father gave to us."

Though most of us will not have to endure the horrors of a holocaust, life is a war. Whether a person knows Christ or not, life is full of trouble. Even when we reach the height of invincible love, we are still in this world and we will still have tears, pain, and death. But in the midst of that, a woman can have peace, because she knows she is His beloved princess. We also know that one day He will come thundering through the sky to take us to a place where there is no more crying, no more sorrow, and no more death.

And in the meantime, no mountain will ever be high enough to keep God from getting to us. Paul states:

Who shall separate us from the love of Christ? Shall trouble or hardship or persecution or famine or nakedness or danger or sword?

No, in all these things we are more than conquerors through him who loved us. (Romans 8:35, 37)

Be still and know that He is God. He will come to us, letting us know that we are loved.

Ain't No Mountain High Enough

In the midst of sorrow, Jesus calls to us, "Principessa!" His melody cannot die, for He is alive and He plays it softly to bring hope to our hearts, even in the bleakest of situations. He longs to protect us and give us hope. He gave His life for us. He couldn't bear to spend eternity without us. It is because of His mercies that we are not consumed, and morning by morning we hear His voice, saying, "Good morning, princess!"

As Benigni played the music for his wife, I (Dee) was reminded of the times in my life when I was desperate: when my Dad was having triple bypass surgery and I feared he didn't know the Lord; when our son was rebelling against the Lord; when I felt betrayed by one I thought would never betray me. I (Kathy) remember the time in my life when I was in such despair that I lay on a couch for three days and just didn't want to get up; when my mom was dying; when I felt at the end of my rope in my career.

Somehow or other, the Lord always finds a way to comfort us, to play the music for us.

Sometimes it is through His presence, so real, so tangible. Recently, I (Kathy) was home in Long Island, dealing with a fresh disappointment in my life. Curling up, I put my head on my pillow and wept. All of a sudden I felt like I was resting my head on Jesus' lap. I could almost feel His tender hands gently stroking my hair. I knew He was wiping my tears. He'd heard my prayers.

Other times, Jesus plays the music for us through friends. Once as I was listening with friends to sermon tapes on the Song of Songs, I found myself wondering: *If I never get married, if I don't experience becoming one with a man, when I stand before Jesus, will I have missed something? Will I have missed the greatest love?* I ended up calling Allyson and going on and on about love and relationships and marriage. She let me rant and rave a little bit, and when I was done pontificating, her simple answer silenced me. "Kathy, my Bible says that the greatest love that a man could have is to lay down his life for his friends." Allyson has experienced both career and family and has one of the best marriages I've seen. So for her to say that meant so much. And then, she said, earnestly:

> Kathy, you are loved. Not in the context of marriage, but by your friends,
> by your extended family, and by such an arena of people. Your audience,
> the women you speak to, love you—I can see it on their faces. You love
> them, and they love you.

At that point I was able to hear the music through my friend. And I can
honestly say today that although I've had periods in my life when I long for
a husband and I anxiously await his arrival, I have reached a point of having a particular joy in my singleness. There are even some days when I consider it a gift. If God is truly sovereign, and I believe He is, then whatever
stage we are in in life is exactly where God has allowed us to be. His hand
most definitely can be in someone getting married, and His hand most definitely can be in someone being single. We must remember that there are
different stages in life. It's important not to despise where God has placed
you. If you are truly in the palm of His hands, then He has not left you. He
is with you. We need to be thankful for the profound simplicity of that fact.
The Lord truly has allowed me to become contented in my singleness. So
often I meet other single men and women who are so discontent. It's almost
as if they're floating through life in a holding pattern waiting for the day
when they can truly soar. God says I can fly like an eagle. The Kingdom of
God is at hand. So much work to be done. And most of all, so much joy in
experiencing intimacy with Jesus and splashing that love onto the world.
We can trust Him. He holds our future. He knows what we need.

God brought Ruth a husband. He allowed Naomi to stay single. But
for both, He played the music.

I Write the Songs

Naomi has often been called a female version of Job. She suffered so
much. The opening six verses in the Book of Ruth are one piercing arrow
after another into Naomi's heart.

- A famine comes to Bethlehem

- The family moves to idol-worshipping Moab

- Naomi's husband dies

- Her sons marry pagan Moabite women

- The daughters-in-law are barren; there are no grandbabies bouncing on her knees

- The sons die

Naomi is completely devastated. She turns away from Moab, away from the land of her losses, and walks, like an empty husk, home, toward Bethlehem. She is without a husband, without sons, without hope.

Yet a faint strain of music begins at this point in the story. Her daughters-in-law love Naomi so much that they are willing to leave their own land, their own people, and their own mothers just to be with her. It is a sweet song, orchestrated by God. But Naomi cannot hear it. She turns to Orpah and Ruth and says:

Go back, each of you, to your mother's home. (Ruth 1:8)

The music plays again, this time slightly louder. The girls weep, cling to her, and cry:

We will go back with you to your people. (Ruth 1:10)

Still, Naomi cannot hear the violins. Again, she sends the girls back. In an impassioned speech, she tells them she is empty, without anything to offer them. Practically shaking her fist at heaven she cries:

Return home, my daughters. Why would you come with me? Am I going to have any more sons, who could become your husbands? Return home, my daughters; I am too old to have another husband. Even if I thought there was still hope for me—even if I had a husband tonight and then gave birth to sons—would you wait until they grew up? Would you remain unmarried for them? No, my daughters. It is more bitter for me than for you, because the Lord's hand has gone out against me! (Ruth 1:11–13)

At this point Orpah kisses her mother-in-law good-bye and retreats. She is frightened. She is unwilling to die to herself. She does not believe there will be a resurrection. And we never hear another word about Orpah.

Naomi turns to Ruth and, for the fourth time, sends her back:

Look, . . . your sister-in-law is going back to her people and her gods. Go back with her. (Ruth 1:15)

The orchestra swells as Ruth falls to her knees, clings to Naomi, and makes the speech that has given her a place in history:

Intreat me not to leave thee, or to return from following after thee: for whither thou goest, I will go; and where thou lodgest, I will lodge: thy people shall be my people, and thy God my God: Where thou diest, will I die, and there will I be buried: the LORD do so to me, and more also, if ought but death part thee and me. (Ruth 1:16–17 KJV)

Does Naomi hear the symphony playing? No. She does not.

Does Ruth give up? No. She is faithful and true, patient and loving. It takes a long time for Naomi to hear the music. But finally, she does.

It happens the day Ruth comes home after meeting Boaz, her arms so laden with grain she can hardly walk. Naomi is amazed, and she asks:

Where did you glean today? Where did you work? Blessed be the man who took notice of you! (Ruth 2:19)

Innocently, Ruth says the name that is going to bring hope to Naomi, the name that is going to help Naomi hear the music. Ruth says:

The name of the man I worked with today is Boaz. (Ruth 2:19)

Finally, Naomi hears the music. Out of all the farms in Bethlehem, Ruth "happened" into the field of the man who could truly help them: their kinsman-redeemer. Naomi lifts her eyes toward heaven. For the first time, she hears, "Princess! I have not forgotten you! I am alive. I care about you. I will not leave you destitute."

My Heart Will Go On

Smiling through her tears, Naomi turns to Ruth and says:

He [God] has not stopped showing his kindness to the living and the dead. . . . That man [Boaz] is our close relative; he is one of our kinsman-redeemers. (Ruth 2:20)

The time for sitting around in a slump is over. Naomi flies into action, a matchmaker, giving Ruth elaborate instructions. "Wash yourself! Perfume yourself! Put on your finest garments!"

Got to Get You into My Life

Ruth slips out under the black Bethlehem sky to the place where Boaz is sleeping, guarding the grain. According to Naomi's instructions, she is to approach Boaz quietly, uncover his feet, and lie down next to him.

Strange plan? It surely seems so. But it is filled with beautiful symbolism when you remember that Boaz is a Christ figure. Though Boaz has wooed Ruth, she needs to respond. When Boaz suddenly wakes and sees Ruth there, she says:

I am your servant Ruth. . . . Spread the corner of your garment over me, since you are a kinsman-redeemer. (Ruth 3:9)

Like Ruth, we are destitute and in need of covering. Jesus is our kinsman. He is one of us, related to us, because He was willing to leave His throne in heaven and become a man. He is also our redeemer. Boaz redeemed Ruth with silver and gold, but Jesus redeemed us with His precious blood. Each of us needs to come to Him and say,

> Cover me, cover me. Spread the garment of Your righteousness over me, because You, and You alone, have the power to do so. You are my Kinsman-Redeemer.

If we ask Jesus to do that, He will respond to us the way Boaz responded to Ruth:

> *And now, my daughter, don't be afraid. I will do for you all you ask.* (Ruth 3:11)

Of course, as in any good love story, there are obstacles. But the prince surmounts them. He is on a quest for the princess.

At the close of the Book of Ruth, there is a wedding. Boaz takes Ruth as his wife, and in that union the Lord enables her to conceive.

Though Ruth was a Moabite, belonging to a people who practiced sexual immorality and child sacrifice, all that is in the past. Ruth is a new creation. She is covered. She is whiter than snow. She is remembered for her unfailing love. Through her, the love of God spilled out to the next generation, even to the children yet to be born.

What the World Needs Now

Do you know what the Bible says is the mark of a Christian? Is it our views on abortion or homosexuality? Is it our involvement in a Bible-believing church? Is it our doctrinal stance on salvation?

No. What arrests people, what causes us to stand out from the world, is not our convictions, as important as those may be, it is love. When we can live a life of love, the world sits up and takes notice. When we can overcome our differences, when we can cross the lines of denomination, race, and culture and truly love each other, the world thinks, *Maybe there really is some-thing to Christianity.* Jesus prayed, in His last prayer for us on earth:

> *May they be brought to complete unity to let the world know that you sent me and have loved them even as you have loved me.* (John 17:23)

Francis Schaeffer explained in *The Mark of a Christian* that if we really love each other, the world is drawn to Christ. But if we don't, the world dismisses us as just another club.[1] The reason the early church spread like wildfire was because of the early Christians' love.

Love is the mark of a Christian because God is love. We can't, in the flesh, love those who are hard to love—but God can. Our lack of love, or our lack of gentleness, or our lack of compassion can cling to us like stubborn leaves that cling to branches throughout the fall and winter. It isn't until spring, when the sap rises, that those leaves are finally pushed off. In the same way, we may want, in our flesh, to love somebody who is hard to love, but we just can't. So we earnestly pray that God will fill us with love for that person. Then one day, we realize that His love has had His way in us. The sap has risen and pushed those ugly leaves off. I (Dee) experienced that with our daughter Beth. When we adopted her, as a twelve-year-old, I showed her kindness, but genuine love wasn't really in me. I asked God for it, but I was still so easily irritated with her. And then one day, when someone hurt her feelings because of her missing arm, I became like a mother bear. And I realized, I really love this child. I'm not just showing her love. I love her! And though I can still become irritated with her, there is a genuine change in my attitude toward her. And I have found that as I play games with her, or hide a little surprise under her pillow, or tell her what I like in her, my love for her actually increases. John explains it like this:

> *God is love. Whoever lives in love lives in God, and God in him.* (1 John 4:16b)

And I know, also, that my only hope of embracing my eighty-eight-year-old father with the love of Jesus is to show him that love. When he raises his voice at me (because old age is like walking through a mine-field and he is grieving the loss of health, of friends, of independence . . .), when he is outraged that I insist on driving the car (because he'll kill us all if he drives), when he barks at my grown children to "Get off the phone!" (because they don't know the value of a dollar), I absolutely have to respond in love. I can be firm, but I must be kind. I can disagree, but I must be respectful. I must be the love of Jesus to him. It amazes me that in the midst of these stressful situations, God gives me His peace and perspective. He is helping me to realize how precious Dad is to me—and to remember that one day I, too, may need a whole lot of grace.

I am falling back. He is catching me.

I (Kathy) used to have such a problem with anger. Even my mother, though she mellowed, could get extremely angry and upset about tiny little things. I had such tension with my mother in my teens, and to this day, I could weep about it. One time I even pushed her up against the wall, I was so out of control. She didn't know how to handle me, and I didn't know how to handle her. Those were not easy times in our lives. I was so unruly, my mother used to have my uncles come and talk to me, since my dad had died. Anger was so ingrained in me that it was my natural response to problems.

When I first met the Lord, it was the start of my praying to be more graceful, gentle, and kind. I yearned to be like some of the women I'd read about in Scripture and some of the women I was meeting who truly clothed themselves in Christ. When I look at myself objectively, I can see how God has done a great work in me. Sometimes I am even shocked at the days and the weeks and the months that go by. Though I can get frustrated, there's not this rage that I used to feel. I'm so much more consistent. Sometimes when I go home to New York I get together with my large extended family. I find myself getting startled when they shout at each other, "Pass the buttah!" That way of communicating, though endearing in those settings, is not the way I live anymore. Those waves of anger that used to come in and destroy everything around me are now so much more subdued. His presence comes over me and checks me. I know I'm a miracle.

Recently I was sitting at an award ceremony and beginning to bristle because I knew the inside scoop on the lives of some of the people getting significant awards of recognition. I was thinking, *Hey, Lord, I don't understand.* And then, God quickly spoke to me: "Kathy, you are not above anything. And you are working through your own pride and sin with Me. It is only by My grace that you have a platform. Please don't forget that." Oh, how I realize it has always got to be about Jesus and not about me. I'm continually learning to live with the attitude of my heart being "You have the speck; I have the log."

One night a friend dragged me to a worship event in Nashville. I say dragged because I was in such a bad state of mind. I was tired of some of the battles in my soul. I was tired of injustices. I was just tired. I sat there with my arms folded, thinking, *Yeah, yeah, yeah, whatever.* They started singing, "My Jesus, My Savior, Lord there is none like You . . ." and I could feel myself starting to melt. I think it's in those times more than ever that I grieve. He's so good and so kind and so gentle. His mercy pours over me as His love embraces me. All my walls come tumbling down, and I see Him clearly. I yearn to be His love to each person who comes across my path.

Kathy wrote "May I Be His Love." I (Dee) think of Ruth every time she sings it.

> May I be His love for you
> May I lift your eyes toward heaven
> May I come to you and lead you to His light
> May I cry His tears for you
> May I be the place that you can run to
> Where you'll hear His voice
> And see Him in my eyes
> All your life
> May I be His love

When Ruth showed Naomi unfailing love, she was breaking her alabaster box at the feet of Jesus. In *Lady in Waiting,* the authors describe Ruth:

She recklessly abandoned herself to the only true God. She willingly broke her alabaster box and followed wherever He would lead her.[2]

It is one thing to make a pledge to the Lord in a single moment and to say, "Wherever You want me to go, Lord, I will go." It is another thing truly to make a lifetime commitment to Him, day after day, often in the mundane. That's what Ruth did. She stayed with Naomi, even when Naomi continued to be ungrateful for her. She ministered to Naomi, day after unappreciated day. What was Ruth's alabaster box? Surely she gave up her own parents, her own land, and her own people. She gave up, or at least she thought she did, her chance for remarrying. She gave up the desire to defend herself when Naomi was ungrateful for her. Box after box she smashed at the feet of the one true God. He enabled Ruth to fill Naomi's empty arms with love, with grain, and finally, with a grandson.

The result? God's love just kept welling up in Ruth. He increased her capacity to love. As she lived in love, she lived in God, and He in her. Every sacrifice Ruth made, God blessed. And her name is recorded in the genealogy of Christ. As with Mary of Bethany, the Lord made sure her sacrifices would not be forgotten.

I've Grown Accustomed to His Face

The face of God shining upon you is like the warmth of the sun on a beautiful day at the beach. One accustomed to that warmth is much more careful not to let the cloud of sin block His face. When Kathy was asked in her interview for *Today's Christian Woman* if she had any struggles, as a single woman, with staying sexually pure, Kathy said, tongue in cheek:

> No. Never. I have no emotions, no hormones, no needs! Next question, please.

The interviewer persisted: "Kidding aside, how do you handle those urges?" Kathy answered:

I think about the consequences. I know all havoc will break loose in my relationship with God and those around me if I choose to disobey God in my sexual desires. Anyone who's come close to crossing that line knows exactly what I'm talking about. Bottom line: Nothing is worth sacrificing God's peace.[3]

Perhaps the same motivation caused Ruth to respond with such love to the hurts Naomi inflicted upon her. She was experiencing the sweet presence of God, the warmth of His face shining upon her. She did not want to walk away from that light. So when she was reviled, she reviled not. She continued, day after day, to live in love.

Isn't She Lovely?

And people all over Bethlehem were talking. When Boaz first met Ruth, he said:

I've been told all about what you have done for your mother-in-law. (Ruth 2:11a)

At the close of the Book of Ruth, when Ruth lays her newborn infant in Naomi's arms, people are talking again. The women of Bethlehem, the same women who heard Naomi disparage Ruth's presence when they arrived in Bethlehem, turn to Naomi and say:

Your daughter-in-law, who loves you . . . is better to you than seven sons.
(Ruth 4:15b)

A perfect family, according to Jewish tradition, was seven sons. But Ruth, because of her amazing love, was better than that. Wouldn't you love it if people would say that about you? It is possible. When you choose to live consistently in the love of God, then that love will be made complete in you.

In marriage, it takes time to trust the heart of your husband. In the early years you are more apt to be hurt by a remark, because you don't completely trust his heart and he doesn't completely know what you need. But if you hang on and continue to love, you are most likely to make it through the wilderness into the land of invincible love. Then, when trouble comes, it doesn't destroy your love, because you know your husband's heart and he knows yours. In the Song of Songs, the Shulammite maiden grows to the point where she can embrace both the sweet south wind and the bitter north wind—for both will spread the fragrance of Christ to the world:

> Awake, north wind,
>> and come, south wind!
> Blow on my garden,
>> that its fragrance may spread abroad. (Song of Songs 4:16a)

She also has the confidence that, no matter what, her love is permanent:

> Many waters cannot quench love;
>> rivers cannot wash it away. (Song of Songs 8:7a)

In the same way, it takes time to know God's heart and to see His goodness, especially in the wilderness. It takes getting quiet in order to hear His music. It takes a childlike trust to hold His hand.

Once we have experienced His faithfulness, we don't want to walk away. Invincible love is not a freedom from trouble but the knowledge that when trouble comes we have not been abandoned or betrayed by God. Perfect love casts out the fear that He has lost control or that He does not care. We know His heart. We know we are His princesses. We know He is coming.

His love is here to stay.

Notes

Chapter 1: A Dream Is a Wish Your Heart Makes

1. *The Visual Bible: The Healing Touch of Jesus,* videotape (Dallas: Visual Entertainment, 1997).

2. Jack Deere, as quoted in Mike Bickle, *Passion for Jesus* (Orlando: Creation House, 1993), 7.

3. Charles Spurgeon, *Spurgeon's Expository Encyclopedia: Sermons by Charles H. Spurgeon,* vol. 5 (Grand Rapids: Baker, 1998), 147.

Chapter 2: Someday My Prince Will Come

1. Patricia Cornwell, *Ruth, A Portrait: The Story of Ruth Bell Graham* (New York: Doubleday, 1997), 76.

2. Brent Curtis and John Eldredge, *The Sacred Romance: Drawing Closer to the Heart of God* (Nashville: Thomas Nelson, 1997), 69–82.

3. Philip Yancey, *Disappointment with God* (Grand Rapids: Zondervan, 1988), 94.

4. Kathy Troccoli, adapted from *My Life Is in Your Hands* (Grand Rapids: Zondervan, 1997), 162–64.

5. Walter Wangerin Jr., *The Book of God: The Bible as a Novel* (Grand Rapids: Zondervan, 1996), 581.

6. John Phillips, *Exploring the Song of Solomon* (Neptune, N.J.: Loizeaux Brothers, 1984), 7.

Chapter 3: Looking for Love in All the Wrong Places

1. Curtis and Eldredge, *The Sacred Romance,* 135.
2. Philip Yancey, *The Bible Jesus Read* (Grand Rapids: Zondervan, 1999), 159.
3. Yancey, *Disappointment with God,* 157–60.
4. Curtis and Eldredge, *The Sacred Romance,* 19.
5. Frank Miller, *MGM Posters* (JG Press, 1998), 88.
6. Margaret Mitchell, *Gone with the Wind,* vol. 2 (Boston: G. K. Hall & Co., 1936), 1434.
7. Ibid., 1559–60.
8. Ibid., 1571–75.
9. *Gone with the Wind,* videotape (Turner Entertainment, 1939).
10. Mary Blye Howe, "The Love of God Is the Lover's Passionate Embrace," *Dallas Morning News,* 5 February 2000, 5G.

Chapter 4: It Had to Be You

1. Elisabeth Elliot, *Let Me Be a Woman: Notes to My Daughter on the Meaning of Womanhood* (Wheaton: Tyndale, 1986), 13.
2. Gene Edwards, *The Divine Romance* (Wheaton: Tyndale, 1993).
3. Charles Spurgeon, *The Treasury of David,* vol. 3, pt. 2 (Peabody, Mass.: Hendrickson, n.d.), 90.
4. Ibid., 263.
5. Leisha Joseph with Deborah Bruner Mendenhall, *Little Girl Lost* (New York: Doubleday, 1998), 2.
6. Curtis and Eldredge, *The Sacred Romance,* 16.
7. Max Lucado, *When Christ Comes: The Beginning of the Very Best* (Nashville: W Publishing, 1999), 145.

Chapter 5: Love Me Tender

1. Sheldon Vanauken, *A Severe Mercy* (New York: Harper & Row, 1977), 25–26, 29.
2. Ibid., 28–29.
3. Jamie Lash, *A Kiss a Day* (Hagerstown, Md.: Ebed, 1996), 17.
4. Ibid., 21.
5. Wangerin, *The Book of God,* 742.
6. Ibid., 741.
7. Charles Swindoll, "Insight for Living," radio brodcast.
8. Curtis and Eldredge, *The Sacred Romance,* 6.
9. Spurgeon, *The Treasury of David,* 84.
10. Max Lucado, *He Still Moves Stones* (Nashville: W Publishing, 1999), 51.

Chapter 6: Killing Me Softly

1. Hannah Hurnard, *Hinds' Feet on High Places* (Wheaton: Tyndale, 1977), 62–63. Unfortunately, after Hannah Hurnard wrote this wonderful classic, she turned away from Christianity into universalism, pantheism, and New Age philosophies. We cannot recommend her subsequent books. However, *Hinds' Feet on High Places* adheres to the Word of God and is a beautiful and true allegory.
2. Ibid., 66.
3. Francine Rivers, *Redeeming Love* (Chicago: Alabaster, 1997), 81.
4. Luis Palau, *The Schemer and the Dreamer: God's Way to the Top* (Grand Rapids: Discovery House, 1999), 9.
5. Leslie Williams, *Night Wrestlings: Struggling for Answers and Finding God* (Dallas: W Publishing, 1997), 14.
6. Leslie Williams, *Seduction of the Lesser Gods: Life, Love, Church, and Other Dangerous Idols* (Nashville: W Publishing, 1997), 12.

Chapter 7: You Can't Hurry Love

1. Charles Spurgeon, *Spurgeon's Expository Encyclopedia*, vol. 3, 455.
2. Elisabeth Elliot, *The Path of Loneliness* (Nashville: Thomas Nelson, 1991), 22.

Chapter 8: Unforgettable

1. Debby Jones and Jackie Kendall, *Lady in Waiting: Developing Your Love Relationships* (Shippensburg, Penn.: Treasure House, 1995), 3.
2. Leon Morris, "John" in *The New International Commentary* (Grand Rapids: Eerdmans, 1971), 576–77.
3. A. B. Bruce, *The Training of the Twelve* (Grand Rapids: Kregel, 1988), 301.
4. www.upa.pdx.edu/sheaj/mteresa, Internet, 20 January 2000.
5. Peggy Noonan, "A Combatant in the World," *Time*, 15 September 1997, 84.
6. Dallas Willard, *The Divine Conspiracy: Rediscovering Our Hidden Life in God* (New York: HarperCollins, 1998), 77.

Chapter 9: Our Love Is Here to Stay

1. Francis A. Schaeffer, *The Mark of a Christian* (Illinois: Inter-Varsity, 1970), 138–39.
2. Jones and Kendall, *Lady in Waiting*, 4.
3. Kathy Troccoli, "Sentimental Journey," *Today's Christian Woman*, November/ December 1999, 142.

Sources for Songs

"A Baby's Prayer" (page 35)
Lyrics by Kathy Troccoli. Copyright © 1996 Sony/ATV Songs LLC. All rights on behalf of Sony/ATV Songs LLC administered by Sony/ATV Music Publishing, 8 Music Square West, Nashville, TN 37203. All rights reserved. Used by permission.

"Only, Always" (page 39)
Lyrics by Kathy Troccoli. Copyright © 1999 Sony/ATV Songs LLC. All rights on behalf of Sony/ATV Songs LLC administered by Sony/ATV Music Publishing, 8 Music Square West, Nashville, TN 37203. All rights reserved. Used by permission.

"Missing You" (page 78)
Lyrics by Chris Rice. Copyright © 1994 BMG Songs, Inc. (ASCAP). BMG Music Publishing, 14000 18th Avenue South, Nashville, TN 37212. All rights reserved. Used by permission.

"Come Away" (page 98)
Lyrics by Amy Shreve. Copyright © 1995 G. B. Wix Publishing (ASCAP). All rights reserved. Used by permission.

"All the Leaves" (page 98)
Lyrics by Amy Shreve. Copyright © 1995 G. B. Wix Publishing (ASCAP). All rights reserved. Used by permission.

"For the Beauty of the Earth" (page 100)
Public domain.

"Break My Heart" (page 129)
Lyrics by Kathy Troccoli. Copyright © 2000 Sony/ATV Songs LLC. All rights on behalf of Sony/ATV Songs LLC administered by Sony/ATV Music Publishing, 8 Music Square West, Nashville, TN 37203. All rights reserved. Used by permission.

"Dancing Me through This Life" (page 141)
Lyrics by Kathy Troccoli. Copyright © 2000 Sony/ATV Songs LLC. All rights on behalf of Sony/ATV Songs LLC administered by Sony/ATV Music Publishing, 8 Music Square West, Nashville, TN 37203. All rights reserved. Used by permission.

"How Would I Know?" (page 150)
Lyrics by Jackie Gouché-Ferris. Copyright © 1997 JAAC Publishing (BMI).

"May I Be His Love" (page 191)
Lyrics by Kathy Troccoli and Madeline Stone. Copyright © 1995 Sony/ATV Songs LLC and We Care Music. All rights administered by Sony/ATV Music Publishing, 8 Music Square West, Nashville, TN 37203. All rights reserved. Used by permission.

Coming June 2001:
The Falling in Love with Jesus Curriculum

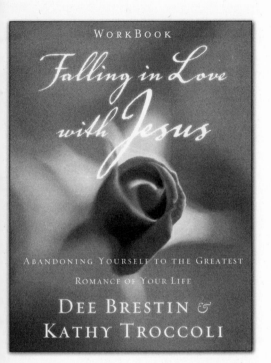

- *Workbook*
- *Facilitator's Guide*
- *Multi-Media Bible Study for Women* (includes: 1 book, 1 workbook, 1 facilitator's guide, 2 videos, and 1 Kathy Troccoli CD, *Love Has a Name*)

Abandon yourself to the greatest romance of your life.

This in-depth Bible Study gives women the inspiration to rethink their relationships with Christ, and to understand and surrender to Him in a fresh new way. Especially geared toward small group study, the *Falling in Love with Jesus* workbook and multi-media study offer humor, wisdom, and stories of women who've experienced a deeper, more passionate relationship with Christ. Ten lessons are divided into 50 days, five days per week, of Scriptures that focus on our love relationship with Jesus, deepening our confidence that we are the object of Christ's affection.

 W PUBLISHING GROUP
www.wpublishinggroup.com

Meditations for Healing

Larry Moen

NEW LEAF
distributing company

Lithia Springs, Georgia

Cover Art: Charles Frizzell © "Ethereal Journey"

Illustrations: Patty Smith

Printed in the United States of America.

Library of Congress Cataloging-in-Publication Data

Meditations for Healing/ [edited by] Larry Moen
p.   cm.
Revised edition of: Guided imagery, v. 2.
ISBN 0-9627209-2-5
1. Meditation. 2. Imagery (Psychology) 3. Visualization.
4. Self-actualization (Psychology) I. Moen, Larry, 1948-.
II. Guided imagery.
BF637.M4G85   1994
153.3'2 — dc20   93-34926
                                                            CIP